Based on the Texas Essential Knowledge and Skills (TEKS)

STAAR

SUCCESS STRATEGIES
Grade 7
Mathematics

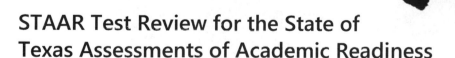

STAAR Test Review for the State of
Texas Assessments of Academic Readiness

Dear Future Exam Success Story:

First of all, **THANK YOU** for purchasing Mometrix study materials!

Second, congratulations! You are one of the few determined test-takers who are committed to doing whatever it takes to excel on your exam. **You have come to the right place.** We developed these study materials with one goal in mind: to deliver you the information you need in a format that's concise and easy to use.

In addition to optimizing your guide for the content of the test, we've outlined our recommended steps for breaking down the preparation process into small, attainable goals so you can make sure you stay on track.

We've also analyzed the entire test-taking process, identifying the most common pitfalls and showing how you can overcome them and be ready for any curveball the test throws you.

Standardized testing is one of the biggest obstacles on your road to success, which only increases the importance of doing well in the high-pressure, high-stakes environment of test day. Your results on this test could have a significant impact on your future, and this guide provides the information and practical advice to help you achieve your full potential on test day.

Your success is our success

We would love to hear from you! If you would like to share the story of your exam success or if you have any questions or comments in regard to our products, please contact us at **800-673-8175** or **support@mometrix.com**.

Thanks again for your business and we wish you continued success!

Sincerely,
The Mometrix Test Preparation Team

Need more help? Check out our flashcards at: http://MometrixFlashcards.com/STAAR

TABLE OF CONTENTS

Introduction

Thank you for purchasing this resource! You have made the choice to prepare yourself for a test that could have a huge impact on your future, and this guide is designed to help you be fully ready for test day. Obviously, it's important to have a solid understanding of the test material, but you also need to be prepared for the unique environment and stressors of the test, so that you can perform to the best of your abilities.

For this purpose, the first section that appears in this guide is the **Success Strategies**. We've devoted countless hours to meticulously researching what works and what doesn't, and we've boiled down our findings to the five most impactful steps you can take to improve your performance on the test. We start at the beginning with study planning and move through the preparation process, all the way to the testing strategies that will help you get the most out of what you know when you're finally sitting in front of the test.

We recommend that you start preparing for your test as far in advance as possible. However, if you've bought this guide as a last-minute study resource and only have a few days before your test, we recommend that you skip over the first two Success Strategies since they address a long-term study plan.

If you struggle with **test anxiety**, we strongly encourage you to check out our recommendations for how you can overcome it. Test anxiety is a formidable foe, but it can be beaten, and we want to make sure you have the tools you need to defeat it.

Success Strategy #1 – Plan Big, Study Small

There's a lot riding on your performance. If you want to ace this test, you're going to need to keep your skills sharp and the material fresh in your mind. You need a plan that lets you review everything you need to know while still fitting in your schedule. We'll break this strategy down into three categories.

Information Organization

Start with the information you already have: the official test outline. From this, you can make a complete list of all the concepts you need to cover before the test. Organize these concepts into groups that can be studied together, and create a list of any related vocabulary you need to learn so you can brush up on any difficult terms. You'll want to keep this vocabulary list handy once you actually start studying since you may need to add to it along the way.

Time Management

Once you have your set of study concepts, decide how to spread them out over the time you have left before the test. Break your study plan into small, clear goals so you have a manageable task for each day and know exactly what you're doing. Then just focus on one small step at a time. When you manage your time this way, you don't need to spend hours at a time studying. Studying a small block of content for a short period each day helps you retain information better and avoid stressing over how much you have left to do. You can relax knowing that you have a plan to cover everything in time. In order for this strategy to be effective though, you have to start studying early and stick to your schedule. Avoid the exhaustion and futility that comes from last-minute cramming!

Study Environment

The environment you study in has a big impact on your learning. Studying in a coffee shop, while probably more enjoyable, is not likely to be as fruitful as studying in a quiet room. It's important to keep distractions to a minimum. You're only planning to study for a short block of time, so make the most of it. Don't pause to check your phone or get up to find a snack. It's also important to **avoid multitasking**. Research has consistently shown that multitasking will make your studying dramatically less effective. Your study area should also be comfortable and well-lit so you don't have the distraction of straining your eyes or sitting on an uncomfortable chair.

The time of day you study is also important. You want to be rested and alert. Don't wait until just before bedtime. Study when you'll be most likely to comprehend and remember. Even better, if you know what time of day your test will be, set that time aside for study. That way your brain will be used to working on that subject at that specific time and you'll have a better chance of recalling information.

Finally, it can be helpful to team up with others who are studying for the same test. Your actual studying should be done in as isolated an environment as possible, but the work of organizing the information and setting up the study plan can be divided up. In between study sessions, you can discuss with your teammates the concepts that you're all studying and quiz each other on the details. Just be sure that your teammates are as serious about the test as you are. If you find that your study time is being replaced with social time, you might need to find a new team.

Success Strategy #2 – Make Your Studying Count

You're devoting a lot of time and effort to preparing for this test, so you want to be absolutely certain it will pay off. This means doing more than just reading the content and hoping you can remember it on test day. It's important to make every minute of study count. There are two main areas you can focus on to make your studying count:

Retention

It doesn't matter how much time you study if you can't remember the material. You need to make sure you are retaining the concepts. To check your retention of the information you're learning, try recalling it at later times with minimal prompting. Try carrying around flashcards and glance at one or two from time to time or ask a friend who's also studying for the test to quiz you.

To enhance your retention, look for ways to put the information into practice so that you can apply it rather than simply recalling it. If you're using the information in practical ways, it will be much easier to remember. Similarly, it helps to solidify a concept in your mind if you're not only reading it to yourself but also explaining it to someone else. Ask a friend to let you teach them about a concept you're a little shaky on (or speak aloud to an imaginary audience if necessary). As you try to summarize, define, give examples, and answer your friend's questions, you'll understand the concepts better and they will stay with you longer. Finally, step back for a big picture view and ask yourself how each piece of information fits with the whole subject. When you link the different concepts together and see them working together as a whole, it's easier to remember the individual components.

Finally, practice showing your work on any multi-step problems, even if you're just studying. Writing out each step you take to solve a problem will help solidify the process in your mind, and you'll be more likely to remember it during the test.

Modality

Modality simply refers to the means or method by which you study. Choosing a study modality that fits your own individual learning style is crucial. No two people learn best in exactly the same way, so it's important to know your strengths and use them to your advantage.

For example, if you learn best by visualization, focus on visualizing a concept in your mind and draw an image or a diagram. Try color-coding your notes, illustrating them, or creating symbols that will trigger your mind to recall a learned concept. If you learn best by hearing or discussing information, find a study partner who learns the same way or read aloud to yourself. Think about how to put the information in your own words. Imagine that you are giving a lecture on the topic and record yourself so you can listen to it later.

For any learning style, flashcards can be helpful. Organize the information so you can take advantage of spare moments to review. Underline key words or phrases. Use different colors for different categories. Mnemonic devices (such as creating a short list in which every item starts with the same letter) can also help with retention. Find what works best for you and use it to store the information in your mind most effectively and easily.

Success Strategy #3 – Practice the Right Way

Your success on test day depends not only on how many hours you put into preparing, but also on whether you prepared the right way. It's good to check along the way to see if your studying is paying off. One of the most effective ways to do this is by taking practice tests to evaluate your progress. Practice tests are useful because they show exactly where you need to improve. Every time you take a practice test, pay special attention to these three groups of questions:

- The questions you got wrong
- The questions you had to guess on, even if you guessed right
- The questions you found difficult or slow to work through

This will show you exactly what your weak areas are, and where you need to devote more study time. Ask yourself why each of these questions gave you trouble. Was it because you didn't understand the material? Was it because you didn't remember the vocabulary? Do you need more repetitions on this type of question to build speed and confidence? Dig into those questions and figure out how you can strengthen your weak areas as you go back to review the material.

Additionally, many practice tests have a section explaining the answer choices. It can be tempting to read the explanation and think that you now have a good understanding of the concept. However, an explanation likely only covers part of the question's broader context. Even if the explanation makes sense, **go back and investigate** every concept related to the question until you're positive you have a thorough understanding.

As you go along, keep in mind that the practice test is just that: practice. Memorizing these questions and answers will not be very helpful on the actual test because it is unlikely to have any of the same exact questions. If you only know the right answers to the sample questions, you won't be prepared for the real thing. **Study the concepts** until you understand them fully, and then you'll be able to answer any question that shows up on the test.

It's important to wait on the practice tests until you're ready. If you take a test on your first day of study, you may be overwhelmed by the amount of material covered and how much you need to learn. Work up to it gradually.

On test day, you'll need to be prepared for answering questions, managing your time, and using the test-taking strategies you've learned. It's a lot to balance, like a mental marathon that will have a big impact on your future. Like training for a marathon, you'll need to start slowly and work your way up. When test day arrives, you'll be ready.

Start with what you've read in the first two Success Strategies—plan your course and study in the way that works best for you. If you have time, consider using multiple study resources to get different approaches to the same concepts. It can be helpful to see difficult concepts from more than one angle. Then find a good source for practice tests. Many times, the test website will suggest potential study resources or provide sample tests.

Practice Test Strategy

When you're ready to start taking practice tests, follow this strategy:

Untimed and Open-Book Practice

Take the first test with no time constraints and with your notes and study guide handy. Take your time and focus on applying the strategies you've learned.

Timed and Open-Book Practice

Take the second practice test open-book as well, but set a timer and practice pacing yourself to finish in time.

Timed and Closed-Book Practice

Take any other practice tests as if it were test day. Set a timer and put away your study materials. Sit at a table or desk in a quiet room, imagine yourself at the testing center, and answer questions as quickly and accurately as possible.

Keep repeating timed and closed-book tests on a regular basis until you run out of practice tests or it's time for the actual test. Your mind will be ready for the schedule and stress of test day, and you'll be able to focus on recalling the material you've learned.

Success Strategy #4 – Pace Yourself

Once you're fully prepared for the material on the test, your biggest challenge on test day will be managing your time. Just knowing that the clock is ticking can make you panic even if you have plenty of time left. Work on pacing yourself so you can build confidence against the time constraints of the exam. Pacing is a difficult skill to master, especially in a high-pressure environment, so **practice is vital**.

Set time expectations for your pace based on how much time is available. For example, if a section has 60 questions and the time limit is 30 minutes, you know you have to average 30 seconds or less per question in order to answer them all. Although 30 seconds is the hard limit, set 25 seconds per question as your goal, so you reserve extra time to spend on harder questions. When you budget extra time for the harder questions, you no longer have any reason to stress when those questions take longer to answer.

Don't let this time expectation distract you from working through the test at a calm, steady pace, but keep it in mind so you don't spend too much time on any one question. Recognize that taking extra time on one question you don't understand may keep you from answering two that you do understand later in the test. If your time limit for a question is up and you're still not sure of the answer, mark it and move on, and come back to it later if the time and the test format allow. If the testing format doesn't allow you to return to earlier questions, just make an educated guess; then put it out of your mind and move on.

On the easier questions, be careful not to rush. It may seem wise to hurry through them so you have more time for the challenging ones, but it's not worth missing one if you know the concept and just didn't take the time to read the question fully. Work efficiently but make sure you understand the question and have looked at all of the answer choices, since more than one may seem right at first.

Even if you're paying attention to the time, you may find yourself a little behind at some point. You should speed up to get back on track, but do so wisely. Don't panic; just take a few seconds less on each question until you're caught up. Don't guess without thinking, but do look through the answer choices and eliminate any you know are wrong. If you can get down to two choices, it is often worthwhile to guess from those. Once you've chosen an answer, move on and don't dwell on any that you skipped or had to hurry through. If a question was taking too long, chances are it was one of the harder ones, so you weren't as likely to get it right anyway.

On the other hand, if you find yourself getting ahead of schedule, it may be beneficial to slow down a little. The more quickly you work, the more likely you are to make a careless mistake that will affect your score. You've budgeted time for each question, so don't be afraid to spend that time. Practice an efficient but careful pace to get the most out of the time you have.

Test-Taking Strategies

This section contains a list of test-taking strategies that you may find helpful as you work through the test. By taking what you know and applying logical thought, you can maximize your chances of answering any question correctly!

It is very important to realize that every question is different and every person is different: no single strategy will work on every question, and no single strategy will work for every person. That's why we've included all of them here, so you can try them out and determine which ones work best for different types of questions and which ones work best for you.

Question Strategies

Read Carefully

Read the question and answer choices carefully. Don't miss the question because you misread the terms. You have plenty of time to read each question thoroughly and make sure you understand what is being asked. Yet a happy medium must be attained, so don't waste too much time. You must read carefully, but efficiently.

Contextual Clues

Look for contextual clues. If the question includes a word you are not familiar with, look at the immediate context for some indication of what the word might mean. Contextual clues can often give you all the information you need to decipher the meaning of an unfamiliar word. Even if you can't determine the meaning, you may be able to narrow down the possibilities enough to make a solid guess at the answer to the question.

Prefixes

If you're having trouble with a word in the question or answer choices, try dissecting it. Take advantage of every clue that the word might include. Prefixes and suffixes can be a huge help. Usually they allow you to determine a basic meaning. Pre- means before, post- means after, pro - is positive, de- is negative. From prefixes and suffixes, you can get an idea of the general meaning of the word and try to put it into context.

Hedge Words

Watch out for critical hedge words, such as *likely, may, can, sometimes, often, almost, mostly, usually, generally, rarely*, and *sometimes*. Question writers insert these hedge phrases to cover every possibility. Often an answer choice will be wrong simply because it leaves no room for exception. Be on guard for answer choices that have definitive words such as *exactly* and *always*.

Switchback Words

Stay alert for *switchbacks*. These are the words and phrases frequently used to alert you to shifts in thought. The most common switchback words are *but, although*, and *however*. Others include *nevertheless, on the other hand, even though, while, in spite of, despite, regardless of*. Switchback words are important to catch because they can change the direction of the question or an answer choice.

Face Value

When in doubt, use common sense. Accept the situation in the problem at face value. Don't read too much into it. These problems will not require you to make wild assumptions. If you have to go beyond creativity and warp time or space in order to have an answer choice fit the question, then you should move on and consider the other answer choices. These are normal problems rooted in reality. The applicable relationship or explanation may not be readily apparent, but it is there for you to figure out. Use your common sense to interpret anything that isn't clear.

Answer Choice Strategies

Answer Selection

The most thorough way to pick an answer choice is to identify and eliminate wrong answers until only one is left, then confirm it is the correct answer. Sometimes an answer choice may immediately seem right, but be careful. The test writers will usually put more than one reasonable answer choice on each question, so take a second to read all of them and make sure that the other choices are not equally obvious. As long as you have time left, it is better to read every answer choice than to pick the first one that looks right without checking the others.

Answer Choice Families

An answer choice family consists of two (in rare cases, three) answer choices that are very similar in construction and cannot all be true at the same time. If you see two answer choices that are direct opposites or parallels, one of them is usually the correct answer. For instance, if one answer choice says that quantity x increases and another either says that quantity x decreases (opposite) or says that quantity y increases (parallel), then those answer choices would fall into the same family. An answer choice that doesn't match the construction of the answer choice family is more likely to be incorrect. Most questions will not have answer choice families, but when they do appear, you should be prepared to recognize them.

Eliminate Answers

Eliminate answer choices as soon as you realize they are wrong, but make sure you consider all possibilities. If you are eliminating answer choices and realize that the last one you are left with is also wrong, don't panic. Start over and consider each choice again. There may be something you missed the first time that you will realize on the second pass.

Avoid Fact Traps

Don't be distracted by an answer choice that is factually true but doesn't answer the question. You are looking for the choice that answers the question. Stay focused on what the question is asking for so you don't accidentally pick an answer that is true but incorrect. Always go back to the question and make sure the answer choice you've selected actually answers the question and is not merely a true statement.

Extreme Statements

In general, you should avoid answers that put forth extreme actions as standard practice or proclaim controversial ideas as established fact. An answer choice that states the "process should be used in certain situations, if..." is much more likely to be correct than one that states the "process should be discontinued completely." The first is a calm rational statement and doesn't even make a definitive, uncompromising stance, using a hedge word *if* to provide wiggle room, whereas the second choice is a radical idea and far more extreme.

Benchmark

As you read through the answer choices and you come across one that seems to answer the question well, mentally select that answer choice. This is not your final answer, but it's the one that will help you evaluate the other answer choices. The one that you selected is your benchmark or standard for judging each of the other answer choices. Every other answer choice must be compared to your benchmark. That choice is correct until proven otherwise by another answer choice beating it. If you find a better answer, then that one becomes your new benchmark. Once you've decided that no other choice answers the question as well as your benchmark, you have your final answer.

Predict the Answer

Before you even start looking at the answer choices, it is often best to try to predict the answer. When you come up with the answer on your own, it is easier to avoid distractions and traps because you will know exactly what to look for. The right answer choice is unlikely to be word-for-word what you came up with, but it should be a close match. Even if you are confident that you have the right answer, you should still take the time to read each option before moving on.

General Strategies

Tough Questions

If you are stumped on a problem or it appears too hard or too difficult, don't waste time. Move on! Remember though, if you can quickly check for obviously incorrect answer choices, your chances of guessing correctly are greatly improved. Before you completely give up, at least try to knock out a couple of possible answers. Eliminate what you can and then guess at the remaining answer choices before moving on.

Check Your Work

Since you will probably not know every term listed and the answer to every question, it is important that you get credit for the ones that you do know. Don't miss any questions through careless mistakes. If at all possible, try to take a second to look back over your answer selection and make sure you've selected the correct answer choice and haven't made a costly careless mistake (such as marking an answer choice that you didn't mean to mark). This quick double check should more than pay for itself in caught mistakes for the time it costs.

Pace Yourself

It's easy to be overwhelmed when you're looking at a page full of questions; your mind is confused and full of random thoughts, and the clock is ticking down faster than you would like. Calm down and maintain the pace that you have set for yourself. Especially as you get down to the last few minutes of the test, don't let the small numbers on the clock make you panic. As long as you are on track by monitoring your pace, you are guaranteed to have time for each question.

Don't Rush

It is very easy to make errors when you are in a hurry. Maintaining a fast pace in answering questions is pointless if it makes you miss questions that you would have gotten right otherwise. Test writers like to include distracting information and wrong answers that seem right. Taking a little extra time to avoid careless mistakes can make all the difference in your test score. Find a pace that allows you to be confident in the answers that you select.

Keep Moving

Panicking will not help you pass the test, so do your best to stay calm and keep moving. Taking deep breaths and going through the answer elimination steps you practiced can help to break through a stress barrier and keep your pace.

Final Notes

The combination of a solid foundation of content knowledge and the confidence that comes from practicing your plan for applying that knowledge is the key to maximizing your performance on test day. As your foundation of content knowledge is built up and strengthened, you'll find that the strategies included in this chapter become more and more effective in helping you quickly sift through the distractions and traps of the test to isolate the correct answer.

Now it's time to move on to the test content chapters of this book, but be sure to keep your goal in mind. As you read, think about how you will be able to apply this information on the test. If you've already seen sample questions for the test and you have an idea of the question format and style, try to come up with questions of your own that you can answer based on what you're reading. This will give you valuable practice applying your knowledge in the same ways you can expect to on test day.

Good luck and good studying!

Mathematics Assessment

Probability and Numerical Representations

Probability

Probability is the chance that something will happen. The probability of an event is the ratio of the number of favorable outcomes to the number of possible outcomes when all outcomes are equally likely.

Determine the probability of winning a single coin toss:

Because there is one favorable outcome of two equally likely outcomes, so the probability of winning a coin toss is ½, or 50%.

Determine the probability of a rolling a multiple of 3 on a die:

Both 3 and 6 are multiples of 3, so there are two favorable outcomes out of six equally likely total outcomes. So, the probability of rolling a multiple of 3 on a die is 2/6=1/3=33.3%.

Determine the probability of randomly picking a green marble from a bag containing 15 blue marbles and 5 green marbles, and the probability of randomly picking a red marble from a bag containing 15 blue marbles and 5 green marbles.

There are five green marbles and fifteen blue marbles in a bag. The probability of picking a green marble is the ratio of green marbles to total marbles, or 520=14=25%.

Because there are no red marbles in the bag, it is not possible to choose a red marble from the bag. Therefore, the probability of choosing a red marble is 0.

<u>Example</u>

An MP3 player is set to play songs at random from the fifteen songs it contains in memory. Any song can be played at any time, even if it is repeated. There are 5 songs by Band A, 3 songs by Band B, 2 by Band C, and 5 by Band D. If the player has just played two songs in a row by Band D,

a) What is the probability that the next song will also be by Band D?

b) What is the probability that the next two songs will both be by Band B?

a) The probability of playing a song by any band is proportional to the number of songs by that band over the total number of songs, or $\frac{5}{15} = \frac{1}{3}$ for Band D. The probability of playing any particular song is not affected by what has been played previously, since the choice is random.

b) Since 3 of the 15 songs are by Band B, the probability that any one song will be by that band is $\frac{3}{15} = \frac{1}{5}$. The probability that two successive events will occur is the product of the probabilities for any one event or, in this case $\frac{1}{5} \times \frac{1}{5} = \frac{1}{25}$.

Tree diagram

Ted picks his clothing in the morning from a selection of 4 pairs of pants and 3 shirts. Draw a diagram to find the sample space of the selection of an outfit consisting of exactly one pair of pants and one shirt.

A tree diagram can be used to find the number of different ways pants and shirts can be selected. This will show the sample space for the selection of an outfit.

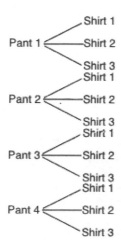

The sample space is the twelve different combinations of pants and shirts.

Sample space, simple event, compound event

Sample space- The set of all outcomes of a probability experiment is called the sample space. For example, if a coin is tossed one time, there are two possible outcomes: heads or tails. So, the sample space consists of two elements. If a coin is tossed two times, there are four possible outcomes: heads then tails, heads then heads, tails then heads, tails then tails. So, the sample space consists of four outcomes.

Simple event- consists of only one outcome in the sample space. For instance, the event of getting heads in a single coin toss is a simple event.

Compound event- consist of more than one outcome in the sample space. For instance, the event of getting heads at least once in two coin tosses is a compound event. The compound event of getting heads is composed of three outcomes: heads then tails, heads then heads, tails then heads.

Theoretical probability vs experimental probability

Theoretical probability is the expected likelihood of an event. Experimental probability is found by conducting trials and comparing the actual occurrence of an event to the number of trials.

For example, the probability of rolling a 2 on a die is 1/6 because there is one favorable outcome, namely rolling a 2, and six equally possible outcomes. So, theoretically, a 2 would appear 100 times if a die is rolled 600 times. Suppose, however, that a die is actually rolled 600 times, and a 2 appears 90 times. The experimental probability is $\frac{90}{600} = \frac{3}{20}$. If the die is a fair die, the experimental probability should closely approximate or equal the theoretical probability when many trials are conducted.

- 13 -

Rational numbers

An integer is a positive whole number, negative whole number, or zero; for example, 8 is an integer. A percent is a part per hundred; for example, 20% is 20 parts per hundred. A fraction is an expression where one number is being divided by another; for example, $\frac{10}{20}$ is a fraction. All rational numbers can be written as a positive or negative whole number, or zero, being divided by another positive or negative whole number. A decimal contains a whole number (or zero), which is to the left of the decimal point, and a portion of a whole number, which is to the right of the decimal point; for example, 20.53 is a number in decimal form. All rational numbers are either terminating decimals, where the numbers to the right of the decimal point end, or repeating decimals, where the numbers to the right of the decimal repeat in a pattern infinitely.

<u>Ordered from least to greatest</u>

Example: Order the following rational numbers from least to greatest: 12%, 1.2, $\frac{1}{12}$, 12.

The first step to solve this is to convert all of the rational numbers in to a common form. For this example we will use decimal form. The 12% as a decimal would be 0.12, and the $\frac{1}{12}$ as a decimal would be ~0.083. The 1.2 and 12 are already in this form. The next step is to then arrange them from least to greatest, which is .083, .12, 1.2, and 12. After they are arranged in the correct order they can be converted back to the original form. So the final answer would be:

From least to greatest: $\frac{1}{12}$, 12%, 1.2, 12.

Converting

As discussed above rational numbers can come in several forms. It will be important to be able to convert rational numbers between forms.

<u>Example 1</u>

Convert each quantity below. Identify the form of each given quantity and describe the new form of the quantity.

a) Write 0.25 as a fraction.

b) Write 0.4 as a percent.

a) 0.25 is a decimal number. A fraction is an expression where one number is being divided by another. To write a decimal number as a fraction, count the number of places right of the decimal. Write a 1 followed by as many zeros as there are decimal places. The fraction will be the decimal number written without a decimal point divided by the number written in the previous step. The fraction can then be reduced by dividing the top and bottom by the same number.

$$0.25 = \frac{25}{100} = \frac{1}{4}$$

b) 0.4 is a decimal. A percent is a part per hundred. To write a decimal as a percent, move the decimal place two digits to the right.

0.4 = 40%

Example 2

Convert each quantity below. Identify the form of each given quantity and describe the new form of the quantity.

      a) Write $\frac{3}{4}$ as a decimal.

      b) Write 200% as a whole number.

a) $\frac{3}{4}$ is a fraction. . A decimal contains a whole number (or zero), which is to the left of the decimal point, and a portion of a whole number, which is to the right of the decimal point. In this case there is no whole number so our decimal would be 0.75.

b) 200% is a percent. A whole number is a positive integer or zero. To write a percent as a whole number, first write the percent as a decimal. Move the decimal two places to the left. 200% = 2.00

    If the quantity after the decimal is 0, then the number can be written as a whole number by only writing the whole number portion of the decimal. 2.00 = 2

Multiplication and division of fractions and decimals

Example 1

Write a situation that could be represented by the expression: $11 \cdot 6.2$.

Any situation where there are 11 groups, where each group has a quantity of 6.2, can be represented by the expression: $11 \cdot 6.2$. For example, a teacher orders lunch for herself and her colleagues. There are a total of 11 lunches ordered. The deli charges $6.20 for each lunch. The total cost of the lunches is the product of the number of lunches and the cost of each lunch: $11 \cdot 6.2$.

Example 2

Rewrite each expression using multiplication.

      a) $\frac{a}{b} \div c$
      b) $\frac{1}{a} \div \frac{1}{b}$
      c) $a \div c$
      d) $a \div \frac{b}{c}$

A division expression can be rewritten using multiplication by a reciprocal. The reciprocal of a number is 1 divided by the number.

a) $\frac{a}{b} \div c = \frac{a}{b} \cdot \frac{1}{c}$
b) $\frac{1}{a} \div \frac{1}{b} = \frac{1}{a} \cdot b$
c) $a \div c = a \cdot \frac{1}{c}$
d) $a \div \frac{b}{c} = a \cdot \frac{c}{b}$

Example 3

Evaluate each of the following:

a) $1.2 \cdot \frac{1}{6}$

b) $8 \cdot 0.05$

c) $\frac{3}{5} \div 4$

d) $2.8 \div \frac{2}{9}$

a) To multiply fractions and decimals, first make sure that the numbers are the same form. The answer can be written as either a fraction or a decimal.

$$1.2 \cdot \frac{1}{6} = \frac{6}{5} \cdot \frac{1}{6} = \frac{1}{5} = 0.2$$

b) $8 \cdot 0.05 = 0.40$

c) To divide a fraction by a whole number, rewrite the expression using multiplication.

$$\frac{3}{5} \cdot 4 = \frac{3}{5} \cdot \frac{1}{4} = \frac{3}{20}$$

d) To divide fractions and decimals, first make sure that the numbers are in the same form. The answer can be written as either a fraction or a decimal.

$$2.8 \div \frac{2}{9} = \frac{14}{5} \div \frac{2}{9} = \frac{14}{5} \cdot \frac{9}{2} = \frac{63}{5} = 12.6$$

Addition and subtraction of fractions and decimals

Simplify or evaluate each expression.

a) $\frac{1}{a} + \frac{1}{b}$

b) $7.1 - \frac{3}{4}$

c) $\frac{6}{5} + 0.4$

a) To add two fractions, with two different denominators, first find a common denominator for the two fractions. The product of the two denominators, in this case ab, is a common denominator. Multiply both the numerator and denominator of each fraction by the factor that produces the common denominator.

$$\frac{1}{a} + \frac{1}{b} = \frac{b}{ab} + \frac{a}{ab} = \frac{b+a}{ab}$$

b) To subtract fractions and decimals, first make sure that the numbers are the same form. The answer can be written as either a fraction or decimal. If using fractions, the fractions must have a common denominator.

$$7.1 - \frac{3}{4} = \frac{71}{10} - \frac{3}{4} = \frac{142}{20} - \frac{15}{20} = \frac{127}{20}$$

- 16 -

c)

$$\frac{6}{5} + 0.4 = \frac{6}{5} + \frac{2}{5} = \frac{8}{5} = 1.6$$

Data representation using models

Example problem 1

Represent the following data in a dot plot and find the mode of the data:

The amount of money your friends make babysitting per hour

5, 2, 7, 9, 4, 5, 6, 7, 9, 7

The data is represented in a dot plot below:

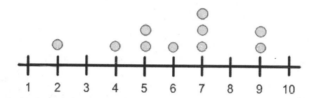

The amount of money your friends make babysitting per hour

This is made by creating a number line that can display the range of data and then placing one dot above each number for each data value equal to that number. The mode of this data is 7, which is the number that occurs in the data most. The mode is easy to see in a dot plot because it is the number that has the most dots. In this data, three people get $7/hour babysitting while only one or two people get paid the other amounts in the list.

Example problem 2

Represent the following data in a box plot:

Michael's math test grades last semester

88, 90, 95, 82, 98, 90, 77, 89, 91

The data is represented in the box plot below:

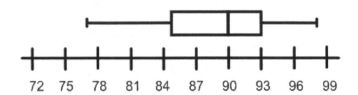

Michael's math test grades last semester

This is made by creating a number line that will fit the distribution of the data and then determining the five points that are needed to create the box plot, which are: the minimum, the maximum, the median, the lower quartile, and the upper quartile. The minimum is the number in the list with the least value, 77, and the maximum is the number with the greatest value, 98. A small tick mark is placed above those two values on the number line. The median of the data is 90, which is found by listing the data in order from least to greatest and finding the number in the middle: 77, 82, 88, 89, 90, 90, 91, 95, 98. The lower quartile is the median of the lower half of the data, which is 85 because the middle of the lower half of the data is between the two middle numbers 82 and 88, and is therefore found by finding their average: $\frac{82+88}{2} = 85$. The upper quartile is the median of the upper half of the data, which is 93 because it is between 91 and 95, and their average is $\frac{91+95}{2} = 93$. A tick mark is placed above the median and upper and lower quartile values on the number line and a box is created around those three marks. A line is then extended from the ends of the box to the minimum and maximum.

Example problem 3

The amount of homework your friends did last night, in minutes, is represented by the following:

45, 25, 33, 65, 37, 55, 45, 42, 31, 49, 48, 22

Represent these data with a histogram.

- 18 -

The histogram below represents the data:

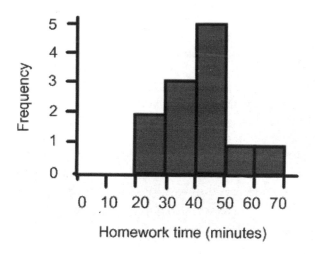

The amount of homework your friends did last night

This is made by creating a graph and labeling the x-axis with homework time, the y-axis with frequency, and creating appropriate intervals for each. (Generally, divide the range of the data into 5 – 7 intervals.) The data values in each interval, which are 10 minute intervals in this histogram, are counted to determine the frequency of data values in those intervals. Adjacent rectangles are created to show the distribution of data. There are 2 pieces of data that fall between 20 and 30 minutes, so that interval has a frequency of 2. There are 3 pieces of data that fall between 30 and 40 minutes, so that interval has a frequency of 3. There are 5 pieces of data that fall between 40 and 50 minutes, so that interval has a frequency of 5. And there is 1 piece of data each that falls between 50 and 60 minutes and 60 and 70 minutes, so those each have a frequency of one.

Example problem 4

Mr. Smith was deciding which of two intersections to post signs at for his garage sale. He sat at one intersection each day for 30 minute time intervals for two consecutive days. Summarize the meaning of his data recorded below and predict what conclusions he may draw.

Number of cars that drove by

Time	Intersection 1	Intersection 2
7am-7:30	8	1
9am-9:30	10	6
11am-11:30	11	10
1pm-1:30	0	9
3pm-3:30	5	10
5pm-5:30	2	4

Mr. Smith will most likely want to place signs for his garage sale at Intersection 2. This is because over the course of the day that Mr. Smith observed Intersection 2, 40 cars drove by, whereas over the course of the day that he observed Intersection 1, only 36 cars drove by. However, Mr. Smith's data shows observations that might make him choose Intersection 1. For example, Mr. Smith might know that morning hours are usually the busiest for garage sales and thus he might want to put his signs at Intersection 1 because more cars drive through that intersection in the morning hours. But, it seems as though the traffic at Intersection 1 tapers off greatly in the afternoon and Mr. Smith might be more concerned with having the possibility of a steady flow of customers at his garage sale all day.

Example problem 5

The local hospital recorded the lengths of the babies born yesterday, given below. Analyze the data and determine what units were being used in the measurements. With the conclusion justify any changes you would recommend for the collection of the data.

Lengths of Babies

1.5, 1.75, 2, 16, 17.5, 17.5, 18.5, 19, 20, 20, 21, 22

It is clear that there are two different units of measurement being used to measure the lengths of babies. All of the data points between 16 and 22 are reasonable if measured in inches. The data points of 1.5, 1.75, and 2 cannot have been measured in inches and were most likely measured in feet. The data points of 1.5, 1.75, and 2 are reasonable if measured in feet, however all the other pieces of data are not reasonable to have been measured in feet. Therefore, the hospital will need to choose one unit of measure when collecting the data on the lengths of the babies born there. One suggestion would be to measure all babies in inches, and thus change the values of 1.5, 1.75, and 2 in the data to 18, 21, and 24.

Example problem 6

Mr. Gordon is Principal at Detroit's largest Middle School and decided to allow students to choose what time they would eat lunch on a given day. To do this he surveyed a group of students and the data is represented in the histogram below. Principal Gordon concluded that he would allow students to eat at their desired lunch time, 11:00-11:30, because the most students wanted to eat during that time. Explain whether or not Principal Gordon's conclusion was justified based on the data in the histogram.

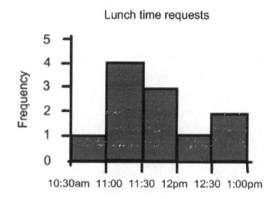

No, Mr. Gordon's conclusion is not justified based on the data given in the histogram. Although the majority of the students he surveyed do want to eat lunch between 11 and 11:30, he only surveyed 11 students. This can be found by adding the frequency of each lunch time period. Surveying a group of 11 students might be a reasonable choice for a very small school, but since Mr. Gordon is the Principal at the largest middle school in Detroit, a sample size of 11 students is not enough to draw justifiable conclusions from. It is possible that the majority of all students will want to each lunch between 11 and 11:30, but Mr. Gordon will need a larger sample size to be able to justify the conclusion that it represents the majority of students' preferences.

Computations and Algebraic Relationships

Problem solving

Example 1

A teacher gives a test with 25 questions. She grades each question. There are 31 students who take the test. Explain which operations are required to find the total number of questions graded.

Each student takes a test containing 25 questions. The teacher grades 25 questions for each student. To find the total number of questions graded, find the product of the number of questions per test and the number of students:

25 questions per student · 31 students = 775 questions

Example 2

There are 24 people in an English class. Miss Foster decides to order three exam books for each student, plus 6 extras. She estimates that she should order 90 exam books. Identify if her solution is reasonable.

- 21 -

Write an expression to determine the total number of exam books to order. Since three books are ordered for each student, first multiply the number of books per student by the number of students: 3 books per student · 24 students = 72 books. Next, add the six extra exam books that Miss Foster would like to order. The total number of books to order is: 72 + 6 = 78 books. Her original estimate of 90 exam books is too large.

Example 3

A car dealer offers two promotions. The first promotion is a discount of 4% off of the car purchase price. The second promotion is $500 cash back. The car Mark is purchasing is $15,000. Explain to Mark which promotion he should choose.

Find the discount to the purchase price with each promotion. For the first promotion, the purchase price is discounted by 4%. To find 4% of the purchase price, multiply the price by 4% as a decimal: 0.04.

$15,000 · 0.04 = $600

The discount to the purchase price with the second promotion is $500, the amount of cash given to the customer. For Mark to receive a greater discount off the purchase price, he should pick the first promotion of 4% off.

Example 4

A map contains a key to relate measurements on the map to real distances. The key on one map says that 2 inches on the map equals 12 miles. Find the distance of a route that is 5 inches long on the map.

Write a proportion that relates the map measurements to real distances. First, write a ratio that relates the information given in the key. The map measurement can be in the numerator, and the real distance in the denominator.

$$\frac{2 \ inches}{12 \ miles}$$

Next, write a ratio relating the known map distance to the unknown real distance. The unknown miles can be represented with the letter m.

$$\frac{5 \ inches}{m \ miles}$$

A proportion is an equation relating two ratios. Write a proportion and solve it for m.

$$\frac{2 \ inches}{12 \ miles} = \frac{5 \ inches}{m \ miles}$$
$$2m = 60$$
$$m = 30$$

The route is 30 miles long.

Unit rate

Unit rate expresses a quantity of one thing in terms of one unit of another. For example, if you travel 30 miles every two hours, a unit rate expresses this comparison in terms of one hour: in one hour you travel 15 miles, so your unit rate is 15 miles per hour. Other examples are how much one ounce of food costs (price per ounce), or figuring out how much one egg costs out of the dozen (price per 1 egg, instead of price per 12 eggs). The denominator of a unit rate is always 1. Unit rates are used to compare different situations to solve problems. For example, to make sure you get the best deal when deciding which kind of soda to buy, you can find the unit rate of each. If Soda #1 costs $1.50 for a 1-liter bottle, and soda #2 costs $2.75 for a 2-liter bottle, it would be a better deal to buy Soda #2, because its unit rate is only $1.375 per 1-liter, which is cheaper than Soda #1. Unit rates can also help determine the length of time a given event will take. For example, if you can paint 2 rooms in 4.5 hours, you can determine how long it will take you to paint 5 rooms by solving for the unit rate per room and then multiplying that by 5.

<u>Example problem 1</u>

At the store you see two different bags of candy for sale. Bag A has 32 pieces of candy in it and costs $2.10. Bag B has 50 pieces of candy in it and costs $3.50. Find the unit cost per one piece of candy from each bag and determine which is the better deal.

One piece of candy in Bag A costs about $0.065, or 6.5 cents. This can be found be taking the total price, $2.10, and dividing it by the number of pieces of candy, 32, to determine the cost for one piece of candy: $\frac{2.10}{32} = 0.06562$, or about $0.065. One piece of candy in Bag B costs $0.07, or 7 cents. This can be found in the same way, dividing the total cost, $3.50, by the number of pieces of candy, 50: $\frac{3.5}{50} = 0.07$, or $0.07. Since a piece of candy in Bag B is slightly more expensive, it is the better deal to buy Bag A.

<u>Example problem 2</u>

You decide to bake oatmeal cookies for a bake sale. Your recipe calls for 5 cups of flour, 2 cups of sugar, 1 cup of butter, and 3 cups of oats. However, you only have 1 cup of oats. You decide to make as many cookies as you can with the 1 cup of oats that you have. Find how much of each ingredient you will need to make that many cookies.

You will need to use $1\,^2/_3$ cups of flour, $^2/_3$ cup of sugar, and $^1/_3$ cup of butter. These can be found by finding the unit rate of each per 1 cup of oats. If there are 5 cups of flour needed for every 3 cups of oats, then $\frac{5}{3} = 1\,^2/_3$ cups of flour needed for every 1 cup of oats. Similarly, if there needs to be 2 cups of sugar for every 3 cups of oats, then there needs to be $^2/_3$ cup of sugar for every 1 cup of oats. And finally, if there is 1 cup of butter needed for every 3 cups of oats, then there will need to be $^1/_3$ cup of butter for every 1 cup of oats.

Example problem 3

Janice made $40 during the first 5 hours she spent babysitting. She will continue to earn money at this rate until she finishes babysitting in 3 more hours. Find how much money Janice earned babysitting and how much she earns per hour.

Janice will earn $64 babysitting in her 8 total hours (adding the first 5 hours to the remaining 3 gives the 8 hour total). This can be found by setting up a proportion comparing money earned to babysitting hours. Since she earns $40 for 5 hours and since the rate is constant, she will earn a proportional amount in 8 hours: $\frac{40}{5} = \frac{x}{8}$. Cross-multiplying will yield $5x = 320$, and division by 5 shows that $x = 64$.

Janice earns $8 per hour. This can be found by taking her total amount earned, $64, and dividing it by the total number of hours worked, 8. Since $\frac{64}{8} = 8$, Janice makes $8 in one hour. This can also be found by finding the unit rate, money earned per hour: $\frac{64}{8} = \frac{x}{1}$. Since cross-multiplying yields $8x = 64$, and division by 8 shows that $x = 8$, Janice earns $8 per hour.

Example problem 4

The McDonalds are taking a family road trip, driving 300 miles to their cabin. It took them 2 hours to drive the first 120 miles. They will drive at the same speed all the way to their cabin. Find the speed at which the McDonalds are driving and how much longer it will take them to get to their cabin.

The McDonalds are driving 60 miles per hour. This can be found by setting up a proportion to find the unit rate, the number of miles they drive per one hour: $\frac{120}{2} = \frac{x}{1}$. Cross-multiplying yields $2x = 120$ and division by 2 shows that $x = 60$.

Since the McDonalds will drive this same speed, it will take them another 3 hours to get to their cabin. This can be found by first finding how many miles the McDonalds have left to drive, which is 300 – 120 = 180. The McDonalds are driving at 60 miles per hour, so a proportion can be set up to determine how many hours it will take them to drive 180 miles: $\frac{180}{x} = \frac{60}{1}$. Cross-multiplying yields $60x = 180$, and division by 60 shows that $x = 3$. This can also be found by using the formula $D = r \times t$ (or $Distance = rate \times time$), where $180 = 60 \times t$, and division by 60 shows that $t = 3$.

Unit prices

A supermarket advertises a special price of $3.00 for 5 oranges. The regular price is $2.50 for 4 oranges. Compare the unit prices of sale and regular-priced oranges.

To find the unit price of sale and regular-priced oranges, find the price of one orange, or the price per orange. The price of a single orange can be found by dividing the total price by the total number of oranges.

Sale price: $\frac{\$3.00}{5 \ oranges} = \frac{\$0.60}{1 \ orange}$

Regular price: $\frac{\$2.50}{4 \ oranges} = \frac{\$0.625}{1 \ orange}$

The sale price is: $0.625 – $0.60 = $0.025 less than the regular price.

Percent

Percent is one way of expressing what portion something is out of a whole. You can think of it like dividing the whole into 100 equal parts, called percents. The whole, all 100 parts, is called 100% (read as "one hundred percent"). Half of the whole is half (50) of the parts, so we say it is 50%, and so on. (Percent compares one quantity to another; sometimes neither number is necessarily 'whole' or 'all' of something.) To find what percent one number is of another, divide the first by the second, and multiply the answer by 100. For example, we can use percent to compare a part to a whole by asking how much money someone spends on their housing payment each month out of his or her total amount of money that month. If someone earns $2000 every month and spends $800 of that on their housing payment, then that person spends $\frac{800}{2000} \times (100) = 0.4 \times 100 = 40\%$ of his or her income on housing payments. Another example showing how percent can simply relate two numbers is comparing your age to your mother's age. If you are 12 years old and your mother is 40 years old, then you are $\frac{12}{40} \times 100 = 0.3 \times 100 = 30\%$ of her age.

Example problem 1

Johnny got 80% of the questions correct on his math test. Find how many questions Johnny answered correctly if the test had 75 questions on it. Also, find what Johnny's new score would be if he was able to earn an extra 10% of his original score by doing corrections on the questions he missed.

Johnny got 60 questions correct. To find this, set up the percent calculation, leaving the number Johnny got right as x: ($\frac{x}{75} \times 100 = 80\%$. Multiply both sides by 75 and then divide both sides by 100 to solve for $x = \frac{80 \times 75}{100} = 60$. We say we are finding 80% of 75, which we now know means simply multiplying 75 by 0.80, which is 60.

Johnny's new score would be $^{66}/_{75}$, which is a score of 88%. This can be found in two ways. One is finding what number of questions is 10% of Johnny's original number right, or 10% of 60, which is 6 questions. If Johnny gets those 6 questions added back to his score, he would then have a total of 66 questions correct out of 75, which is $\frac{66}{75}$, which is 0.88, or 88%. The other way is by finding 10% of Johnny's original score of 80% and adding that to his original score: 10% of 80% = $0.10 \times 80\% = 8\%$, and 80% + 8% = 88%.

Example problem 2

A sweater at a local department store is on sale for $33. Find the original price of the sweater if it is marked 40% off the original price.

The sweater was originally $55. To find this, set up a proportion to determine what number 33 is 60% of. We use 60% because if the sweater is 40% *off* we *subtracted* 40% from the price, so we have 60% *left*. The proportion will compare the percent over 100 to 33 over the original price: $\frac{60}{100} = \frac{33}{x}$. Cross-multiplying yields $60x = 3300$, and division by 60 shows that $x = 55$.

Graphing data from a table

Pairs of socks are sold in packages of 4, 8, 12, and 20. Each pair of socks costs $1.50. Create a graph showing the cost of each package size. The cost of each package size is the cost per pair of socks times the number of socks in the package. A table can be used to organize the information.

Number of pairs	Total cost
4	4 · $1.50 = $6.00
8	8 · $1.50 = $12.00
12	12 · $1.50 = $18.00
20	20 · $1.50 = $30.00

On the graph, let the x-axis be the number of pairs of socks, and the y-axis be the cost of the pairs of socks.

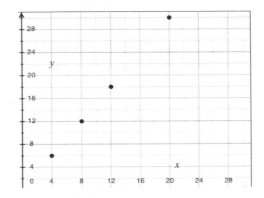

Formulating problem situations and equations

<u>Example 1</u>

The scale below is balanced. The small blocks each weigh 2 pounds. The large blocks each weigh p pounds.

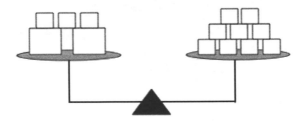

Find the weight of the large cubes.

> Given that the two sides of the scale are equal, write an equation relating the blocks on each side of the scale. Represent the weight of each large block with a p, and the weight of each small block is 2 pounds.

$2 + 2 + 2 + p + p = 2 + 2 + 2 + 2 + 2 + 2 + 2 + 2 + 2$
Simplify each side of the equation.
$6 + 2p = 18$
Subtract 6 from both sides of the equation.
$2p = 12$
Divide both sides of the equation by 2.

- 26 -

$p = 6$

The weight of each large cube, p, is 6 pounds.

Example 2

Write a situation that can be represented using the equation: $3x - 5 = 7$.

Any situation, where an unknown quantity is being multiplied by a factor of three, then five is subtracted from the product, and it is known that this value equals 17, can be represented by the equation: $3x - 5 = 20$. For example, Amelia buys three notebooks. She receives a $5.00 discount on her purchase. The total cost for the three notebooks is $7.00. If she cannot recall the price of each notebook, let x represent the price of each notebook. The total price of the notebooks would be represented by the equation: $3x - 5 = 7$.

Example 3

Write an algebraic expression to determine the nth term of the arithmetic sequence:

31, 25, 19, 13, ...

To find the nth term, find the common difference between each pair of given terms.

2nd term – 1st term: $25 - 31 = -6$
3rd term – 2nd term: $19 - 25 = -6$
4th term – 3rd term: $13 - 19 = -6$

The first term is 31, so when $n = 1$, the term is 31.

1st term: $31 + -6(n - 1)$

Simplify this expression and check it for terms 2, 3, and 4 by evaluating the expression at $n = 2$, 3, and 4.

$31 + -6(n - 1) = 31 - 6n + 6 = -6n + 37$
2nd term: $-6(2) + 37 = -12 + 37 = 25$
3rd term: $-6(3) + 37 = -18 + 37 = 19$
4th term: $-6(4) + 37 = -24 + 37 = 13$

The nth term of the arithmetic sequence is $-6n + 37$.

Geometry and Measurement

Similar triangles

Two triangles that are similar have side lengths that are proportional. For example, triangles ABC and DEF are similar. The length of each side in triangle DEF is 3 times the side length of the corresponding side in triangle ABC. The corresponding angle measures of each triangle are congruent.

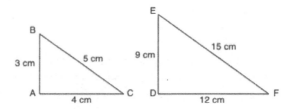

Rectangular prism

Sophia is covering a rectangular prism-shaped couch cushion with fabric. She will be covering all sides of the cushion. The cushion is 4 inches high, 20 inches wide, and 32 inches deep. Draw a diagram to represent the cushion.

A rectangular prism is a three-dimensional figure with rectangular faces. Opposite sides are parallel and congruent. Label the dimensions as given in the problem.

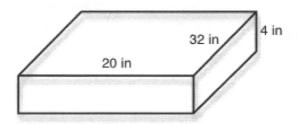

Area

Leslie decides to tile her bathroom floor with tiles that are rectangles. Each rectangle has a length of 10 inches and a width of 8 inches. Find the number of tiles needed for a floor with an area of 3600 in².

First, find the area of each tile. The area of a rectangle is: *lw*, where *l* is the length of the rectangle, and *w* is the width. The area of each tile is: 10 in · 8 in = 80 in². To find the number of tiles needed, divide the total area of the floor, 3600 in², by the area of each tile: 3600 in² ÷ 80 in² = 45. Leslie needs 45 tiles.

Volume

The volume of an object is the amount of space that the object occupies, or is contained within the object.

Example 1

Draw a figure with the following volume: $V = \pi r^2 h$, where r is radius and h is height.

The volume of a cylinder is: $V = \pi r^2 h$.

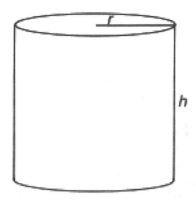

Example 2

Draw a figure with the following volume: $V = \frac{1}{2}bhl$, where b is triangle base length, h is triangle height, and l is length.

The volume of a triangular prism is $V = \frac{1}{2}bhl$.

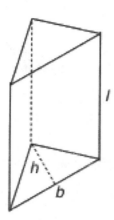

Example 3

Draw a figure with the following volume: $V = lwh$, where l is the length, w is the width, and h is the height.

The volume of a rectangular prism is $V = lwh$.

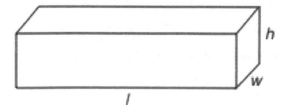

- 29 -

<u>Example 4</u>

A bathtub is approximately shaped like a rectangular prism, with no top. The tub has a length of 60 inches, a width of 24 inches, and a height of 16 inches. The tub is filled halfway with water. Find the volume of the water in the tub.

Drawing a diagram may be helpful. Draw a rectangular prism, with *l* = 60 inches, *w* = 24 inches, and *h* = 16 inches. If the tub is filled halfway, then the height of the water is half of the height of the tub, or 16 inches ÷ 2 = 8 inches. Draw a line representing the fill height of the water.

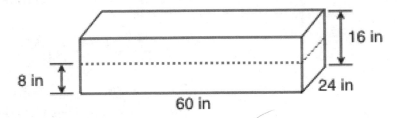

The volume of the water is the volume of the rectangular prism with dimensions: *l* = 60 in, *w* = 24 in, and *h* = 8 in. The volume of a rectangular prism is: *lwh* = 60 in · 24 in · 8 in = 11,520 in³.

Circumference

Steve bakes a cake in a pan with a 9-inch diameter. He decides to decorate the cake by placing raspberries around its edge. Each raspberry has a diameter of approximately 0.5 inches. Use the circumference of the cake to estimate how many raspberries Steve needs to purchase.

It may be helpful to begin with a diagram. Looking at the top of the Steve's cake, the view would be:

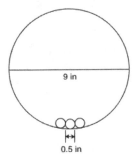

Note that this is not drawn to scale, but is a representation of the problem being solved. To approximate the number of raspberries needed, first find the circumference of the cake. The circumference of a circle is: π*d*, where *d* is the diameter of the circle. The circumference can be calculated 9π = 28.27 inches. To estimate the number of raspberries needed, divide the circumference by the approximate diameter of each raspberry: 28.27 ÷ 0.5 = 56.54. About 56 raspberries will be needed to decorate the cake.

Net of a cylinder

Below is a net of a cylinder. Use the net to determine the surface area and lateral area of the solid.

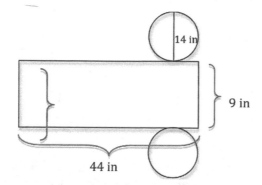

The surface area of the solid is the sum of the areas in the net. Because the figure is a cylinder, the top and bottom of the cylinder are congruent. Both circles will have a diameter of 14. The area of the two circles is: $2(\pi r^2) = 2[\pi(7)^2] = 2\left[\frac{22}{7} \cdot 49\right] = 2(22 \cdot 7) = 2(154) = 308$ in².

The area of the rectangle is: length · width = $9 \cdot 44 = 396$ in².

The surface area is: 308 in² + 396 in² = 704 in²

The lateral area of the solid is the surface area of the solid, excluding the area of the bases. The bases of the cylinder are the two circles, so the lateral area, using the net, would only be the area of the rectangle.

The lateral area is: length · width = $9 \cdot 44 = 396$ in².

Surface area

Example 1

Find the surface area of the figure below. Each triangular face is congruent, and the base is a square.

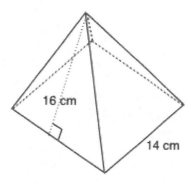

The surface area is the sum of the areas of the faces. The area of the base, which is given as a square, will be the side length squared:

$$a = s^2 = 14^2 = 196 \text{ cm}^2$$

The area of one of the triangular faces will be one half times the height and base of the triangle. The base of the triangle will be one of the sides of the square.

$$a = \frac{1}{2}bh = \frac{1}{2}(14)(16) = 112 \text{ cm}^2$$

There are four triangular faces, so the surface area will be four times the area of the triangular face plus the area of the square base.

$$SA = 4(\text{triangular face area}) + \text{square face area} = 4(112) + 196 = 448 + 196$$
$$= 644 \text{ cm}^2$$

Example 2

Sophia is covering a rectangular prism-shaped couch cushion with fabric. She will be covering all sides of the cushion. The cushion is 4 inches high, 20 inches wide, and 32 inches deep. Determine the area of the fabric needed to cover the cushion.

Drawing a diagram may be helpful. Label the dimensions as given in the problem.

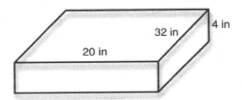

To find the area of fabric needed, find the surface area of the cushion. To find the surface area, sum the areas of each face of the rectangle prism. Opposite faces will have an equal area. The front/back faces of the prism have an area of: 20 in · 4 in = 80 in². The left/right side faces of the prism have an area of: 32 in · 4 in = 128 in². The top/bottom faces of the prism have an area of: 20 in · 32 in = 640 in². The total surface area of the prism, or area of the fabric needed to cover the cushion, is: 80 in² + 80 in² + 128 in² + 128 in² + 640 in² + 640 in² = 1696 in²

Example 3

The lateral surface area is the area around the outside of the sphere. The lateral surface area is given by the formula $A = 4\pi r^2$, where r is the radius. The answer is generally given in terms of pi. A sphere does not have separate formulas for lateral surface area and total surface area as other solid figures do. Often, a problem may ask for the surface area of a sphere. Use the above formula for all problems involving the surface area of a sphere.

The volume is given by the formula $V = \frac{4}{3}\pi r^3$, where r is the radius.

Isometric and front views of three-dimensional figure

The isometric view of a three-dimensional figure is below.

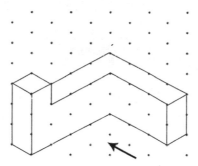

The front view of the object is shown below:

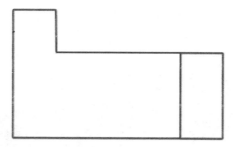

Net of a three-dimensional figure

<u>Example 1</u>

Draw a net of the three-dimensional figure below:

One way to draw a net of the cube is:

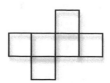

- 33 -

All faces of the cube should be in the net. The two-dimensional net can be folded to construct the original three-dimensional figure.

<u>Example 2</u>

Draw a three-dimensional object that can be constructed using the net below:

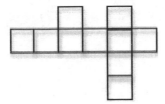

The net can be used to create a rectangular prism. The net would be folded and the resulting figure is:

Data Analysis and Personal Financial Literacy

Bar graph

A bar graph is a frequency plot. It contains the frequency of discrete data values, which can either be numerical or categorical (such as a dollar amount or category types, such as types of books).

Bar graph:

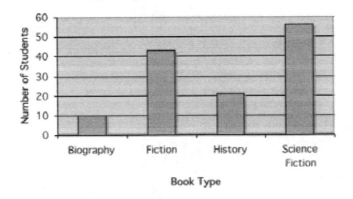

Circle graph

A circle graph shows the relationship between each item in the collected data set to the whole of data that was collected. The circle graph below represents the percentage of the tenth grade that preferred each of the four types of pets. One hundred percent of responses are included in the circle graph.

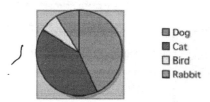

Venn diagram

A Venn diagram uses circles to show the intersection of sets. The example below shows the numbers that are divisible by 2 and 3 between 1 and 20, and the numbers divisible by both in the intersection.

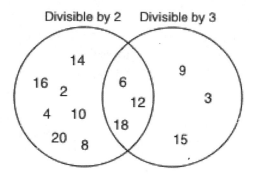

Stem-and-leaf plot

Mr. Glaser records the following grades of students on a 40-point quiz: 18, 27, 29, 30, 34, 35, 35, 37, 40. Represent the data in a stem-and-leaf plot.

The value of the tens place will be the values in the stem, and the value of the ones place will be the values in the leaves. Arrange the values from least to greatest.

stem	leaf
1	8
2	7 9
3	0 4 5 5 7
4	0

Line plot

A line plot contains quantitative (numerical) values on a number line, with an *x* or dot above each value for the number of times that value is present in a sample.

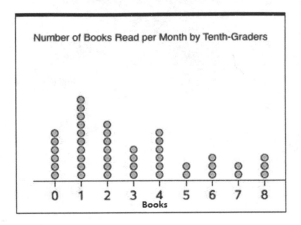

Line graph

A line graph shows the relationship between two quantities. The data points are connected to show the relationship is continuous. The graph below shows the relationship between time, in hours, and distance traveled by car, in miles. The *x*-axis represents time and the *y*-axis represents total distance traveled.

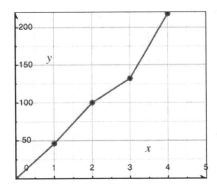

Dot plot, histogram, and box plot

Dot plots, histograms, and box plots are three different methods of representing data sets in graphical form. While they all have similar purposes, some are more suitable for some data sets than others. Dot plots represent each data point as a separate dot, and are most useful for relatively small data sets with a small number of possible values. When the data set contains more than a few dozen points, dot plots may become unwieldy. For larger data sets, where the data distribution is continuous rather than discrete, histograms may be more practical. Histograms are especially useful to estimate the density of the data, and to estimate probability density functions. Box plots may be used to summarize the shape of a larger number of univariate data values; they are most useful for comparing separate groups of data, such as the results of several different experiments, or the statistics of several discrete populations.

Dot plot

A dot plot is a representation of a data set in which each data point is represented by a dot or similar marking, with matching data points grouped in columns. For instance, the data set {2, 1, 3, 1, 1, 5, 4, 4, 3, 3, 3, 4, 1, 5} can be represented as a dot plot as follows:

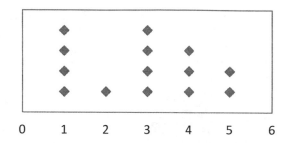

For large data sets, it is possible for each dot in a dot plot to represent more than one data point. However, for such data sets other representations may be more suitable.

Histogram

A histogram is a representation of a data set in which the data are represented by bars corresponding to discrete intervals, with the height of each bar representative of the number of data points falling in the corresponding interval. For example, the data set {101, 141, 105, 159, 122, 107, 145, 153, 183, 172, 164, 162, 144, 132, 138, 116, 155, 147, 141, 129, 168, 145, 152} can be represented by a histogram as follows:

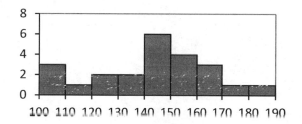

Histograms are useful for large data sets with values that may range continuously over intervals rather than being confined to discrete possibilities.

<u>Box plot</u>

A *box plot*, or box-and-whisker plot, is a representation of one or more data sets in which each data set is represented by a box with a bar in the middle and a "whisker" on each side. The bar represents the *median* of the data, and the edges of the box represent the first and third quartiles. The ends of the whiskers may represent the maximum and minimum data values, although often outliers are excluded and are represented instead as discrete points.

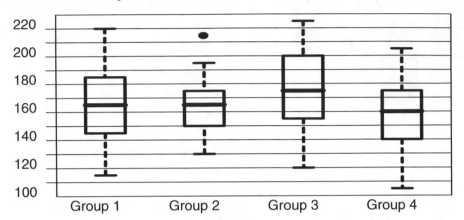

For example, given the data, 5, 5, 6, 9, 12, 14, 15, 17, 17, 21, 24, 26, 29, 31, 36, 38, 39, 46, 47, 49, the following summary statistics may be recorded: Median = 22.5, Q1 = 13, Q3 = 37, minimum = 5, and maximum = 49. Thus, a box plot of this data will show a box, with a middle bar at the value, 22.5, edges of the box at the values, 13 and 37, and whiskers at the values, 5 and 49. Box plots are useful when it is desired to compare the statistics of multiple related data sets, such as several different groups of experimental subjects.

Mathematics Practice Test #1

1. Ana has completed approximately $\frac{2}{7}$ of her research paper. Which of the following best represents the percentage of the paper she has completed?
   - a. 24%
   - b. 26%
   - c. 27%
   - d. 29%

2. What is the square root of the area represented in the model below?

   - a. 3
   - b. 12
   - c. 4
   - d. 16

3. A mathematics test has a 4:2 ratio of data analysis problems to algebra problems. If the test has 18 algebra problems, how many data analysis problems are on the test?
   - a. 24
   - b. 36
   - c. 38
   - d. 28

4. Elijah has prepared $2\frac{1}{2}$ gallons of lemonade to distribute to guests at a party. If there are 25 guests, how much lemonade is available to each guest, given that each guest receives an equal amount?
   - a. $\frac{1}{8}$ of a gallon
   - b. $\frac{1}{6}$ of a gallon
   - c. $\frac{1}{12}$ of a gallon
   - d. $\frac{1}{10}$ of a gallon

5. Which of the following is equivalent to $4^3 + 12 \div 4 + 8^2 \times 3$?
   - a. 249
   - b. 393
   - c. 211
   - d. 259

6. The original price of a jacket is $36.95. The jacket is discounted by 25%. Before tax, which of the following best represents the cost of the jacket?

    a. $27.34
    b. $27.71
    c. $28.82
    d. $29.56

7. A car dealership is having a blowout sale. Douglas finds a car sale-priced at $36,549.15. The car was originally priced at $42,999. What percentage discount would Douglas receive?

    a. 12%
    b. 15%
    c. 18%
    d. 20%

8. A bottle of lotion contains 20 fluid ounces and costs $3.96. Which of the following best represents the cost per fluid ounce?

    a. $0.18
    b. $0.20
    c. $0.22
    d. $0.24

9. Triangle A has side lengths of 12 cm, 8 cm, and 16 cm. Triangle B is related to Triangle A by a scale factor of $\frac{1}{4}$. Which of the following represents the dimensions of Triangle B?

    a. 4 cm, 2 cm, 8 cm
    b. 2 cm, 3 cm, 8 cm
    c. 3 cm, 2 cm, 4 cm
    d. 6 cm, 4 cm, 8 cm

10. A book has a width of 2.5 decimeters. What is the width of the book in centimeters?

    a. 0.25 centimeters
    b. 25 centimeters
    c. 250 centimeters
    d. 0.025 centimeters

11. The approximate volumes of spheres with different radii are listed in the table below.

Radius	Volume
2	33.49 in^3
4	267.95 in^3
6	904.32 in^3
8	2,143.57 in^3

If the volume of each sphere is equal to some ratio multiplied by the product of the cubed radius and pi (π), what is the ratio?

    a. 4
    b. $\frac{1}{3}$
    c. 3
    d. $\frac{4}{3}$

12. Given the sequence represented in the table below, where n represents the position of the term and a_n represents the value of the term, which of the following describes the relationship between the position number and the value of the term?

n	1	2	3	4	5	6
a_n	5	2	−1	−4	−7	−10

a. Multiply n by 2 and subtract 4
b. Multiply n by 2 and subtract 3
c. Multiply n by −3 and add 8
d. Multiply n by −4 and add 1

13. Given the equation represented by the algebra tiles shown below, where  represents x and ■ represents the positive integer 1, which of the following represents the solution?

a. $x = 6$
b. $x = 9$
c. $x = 3$
d. $x = 12$

14. Kevin pays $12.95 for a text messaging service plus $0.07 for each text message he sends. Which of the following equations could be used to represent the total cost, y, when x represents the number of text messages sent?

a. $y = \$12.95x + \$0.07$
b. $y = \$13.02x$
c. $y = \dfrac{\$12.95}{\$0.07}x$
d. $y = \$0.07x + \$12.95$

15. The cost for different numbers of boxes of doughnuts is shown in the table below:

Number of Boxes (b)	Total Cost (c)
4	$15.00
7	$26.25
12	$45.00
18	$67.50

Which equation can be used to find the cost per box, x? Let c represent the total cost and b represent the number of boxes.

a. $x = bc$
b. $x = \dfrac{b}{c}$
c. $x = \dfrac{c}{b}$
d. $x = c + b$

- 41 -

16. What ordered pair is shown on the graph below?

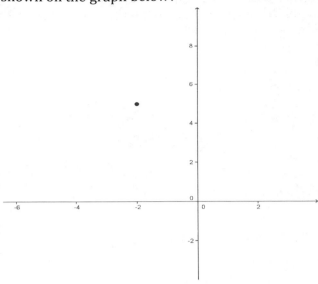

    a. (−2, 5)
    b. (−2, −5)
    c. (2, 5)
    d. (2, −5)

17. A circle has a radius of 23 cm. Which of the following is the best estimate for the circumference of the circle?

    a. 71.76 cm
    b. 143.52 cm
    c. 144.44 cm
    d. 72.22 cm

18. In the formula for the volume of the figure shown below, written as $V = B \cdot h$, h represents the height of the prism when it rests one of its bases. What does the B represent?

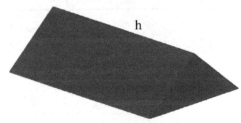

    a. $\frac{1}{3}bh$, where b represents the length of the triangle's base and h represents the triangle's height
    b. bh, where b represents the length of the triangle's base and h represents the triangle's height
    c. $2bh$, where b represents the length of triangle's base and h represents the triangle's height
    d. $\frac{1}{2}bh$, where b represents the length of triangle's base and h represents the triangle's height

19. A rectangular prism has a length of 14.3 cm, a width of 8.9 cm, and a height of 11.7 cm. Which of the following is the best estimate for the volume of the rectangular prism?

    a. 1,512 cm^3
    b. 1,287 cm^3
    c. 1,386 cm^3
    d. 1,620 cm^3

20. A can has a radius of 3.5 cm and a height of 8 cm. Which of the following best represents the volume of the can?

    a. 294.86 cm^3
    b. 298.48 cm^3
    c. 307.72 cm^3
    d. 309.24 cm^3

21. Fred designs a candy box in the shape of a triangular prism. The base of each triangular face measures 4 inches, while the height of the prism is 7 inches. Given that the length of the prism is 11 inches, what is the volume of the candy box?

    a. 102 in^3
    b. 128 in^3
    c. 154 in^3
    d. 308 in^3

22. Miranda rolls a standard die and spins a spinner with 4 equal sections. Which of the following represents the sample space?

    a. 10
    b. 12
    c. 24
    d. 36

23. What is the sample space when flipping three coins?

    a. 6
    b. 8
    c. 12
    d. 15

24. A hat contains 6 red die, 4 green die, and 2 blue die. What is the probability that Sarah pulls out a blue die, replaces it, and then pulls out a green die?

    a. $\frac{1}{18}$
    b. $\frac{1}{3}$
    c. $\frac{1}{2}$
    d. $\frac{1}{16}$

25. The histogram below represents the overall GRE scores for a sample of college students. Which of the following is a true statement?

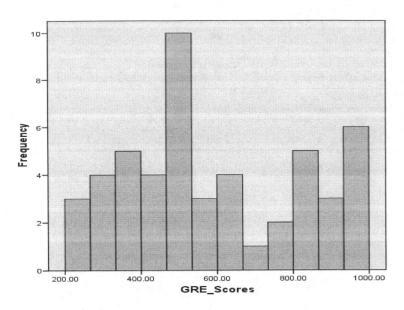

a. The range of GRE scores is approximately 600
b. The average GRE score is 750
c. The median GRE score is approximately 500
d. The fewest number of college students had an approximate score of 800

26. The ages at which a sample of female dogs is spayed is shown below. Based on this sample, what is the average age a female dog gets spayed? 6, 7, 2, 8, 4, 1, 7, 8, 3, 1, 8, 2

a. 3.75
b. 4
c. 4.75
d. 5

27. Amy rolled a die and flipped a coin. What is the probability that she rolled an even number and got heads?

a. $\frac{1}{4}$
b. $\frac{1}{2}$
c. $\frac{3}{4}$
d. $\frac{1}{3}$

28. Which of the following statements correctly describes the relationship between sets and subsets of rational numbers?

a. Natural numbers are a subset of whole numbers.
b. Rational numbers are a subset of integers.
c. Integers are a subset of whole numbers.
d. Rational numbers are a subset of whole numbers.

29. Justin rolls a six-sided die. What is the probability of Justin rolling a number less than 5?

   a. $\frac{2}{3}$

   b. $\frac{1}{3}$

   c. $\frac{5}{6}$

   d. $\frac{1}{2}$

30. A jar is filled with red and green marbles. If the probability of blindly drawing a red marble is $\frac{7}{12}$, what is the probability of blindly drawing a green marble?

   a. $\frac{5}{12}$

   b. $\frac{1}{2}$

   c. $\frac{3}{4}$

   d. $\frac{7}{12}$

31. A survey was conducted to determine which type of pizza a group of 7th grade students preferred. Each student chose only one type of pizza. What is the probability that a student's favorite pizza was sausage?

Pizza Survey				
Cheese	Pepperoni	Sausage	Mushroom	Veggie
48	32	20	12	8

   a. 20

   b. $\frac{1}{6}$

   c. $\frac{1}{20}$

   d. $\frac{1}{5}$

32. What is the constant of proportionality for the data in the table below?

Hours worked	1	2	3	4
Wages ($)	8.50	17.00	25.50	34.00

   a. 17.00

   b. 25.50

   c. 8.50

   d. 34.00

15

33. Which of the following correctly represents the solution to the following inequality on a number line?

$$-2x + 5 > 13$$

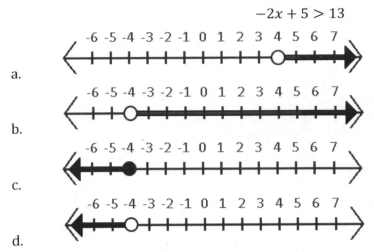

a.

b.

c.

d.

34. Steven has $50 to buy snacks for his party. He plans to spend $10 on soda and the rest on pizza. If each pizza costs $8, which of the following inequalities represent the number (n) of pizzas Steven can buy?

a. $50n \geq 8n - 10$
b. $8n + 10 \leq 50$
c. $10n - 8 \leq 50$
d. $8n \leq 50 - 10n$

35. Which of the following scenarios can be represented by the equation $14 + x = 52$?

a. Stella has $14 in her wallet. How much money does she have if she adds the $52 she earned babysitting last night?
b. Marcus earns $52 mowing yards. How much money does he save if he buys his brother a birthday present that costs $14 and saves the rest?
c. Troy earns $52 working for a neighbor. How much money does he have if he earns an additional $14 working for his aunt?
d. Izzy has $14 of money in her piggy bank. How much money does she have if she adds the $52 she receives for her birthday?

36. Which of the following is the solution to the equation $320 - 12d = 80$?

a. -20
b. 12
c. 20
d. -12

37. Which of the following options makes this inequality a true statement?

$$30b < 372$$

a. $b = 30$
b. $b = 22$
c. $b = 14$
d. $b = 12$

38. Which of the following values of x makes this equation a true statement?
$$-2 - 3x = -14$$

    a. -4
    b. 4
    c. 3
    d. -5

39. If 1 mile = 5,280 feet, which of the following proportions can be used to determine the number of miles equal to 26,400 feet?

    a. $\dfrac{5,280}{1} = \dfrac{26,400}{x}$
    b. $\dfrac{5,280}{1} = \dfrac{x}{26,400}$
    c. $\dfrac{5,280}{x} = \dfrac{26,400}{1}$
    d. $\dfrac{5,280}{26,400} = \dfrac{x}{1}$

40. Which of the following statements is true for this set of similar triangles?

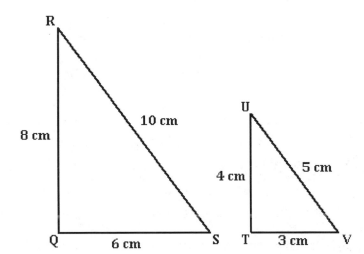

    a. $\dfrac{RQ}{RS} = \dfrac{UT}{TV}$
    b. $\dfrac{RS}{QS} = \dfrac{UV}{UT}$
    c. $\dfrac{QS}{RS} = \dfrac{TV}{UV}$
    d. $\dfrac{RQ}{QS} = \dfrac{UT}{UV}$

41. Which of the following statements is true regarding the circumference (C) and the diameter (d) of a circle?

    a. $\pi = C + d$
    b. $\pi = Cd$
    c. $\pi = \dfrac{C}{d}$
    d. $\pi = \dfrac{d}{C}$

- 47 -

42. Which of the following statements is NOT true about this figure?

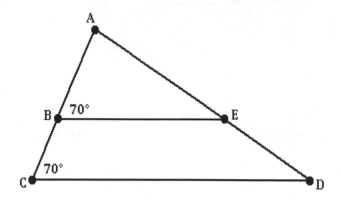

    a. $\triangle ABE$ is similar to $\triangle ACD$
    b. $BE = CD$
    c. $\angle B \cong \angle C$
    d. $\dfrac{AB}{AC} = \dfrac{AE}{AD}$

43. Two rectangles are similar. The length and the width of the first rectangle is 3 meters by 6 meters. The second rectangle is similar by a scale factor of $\frac{1}{2}$. What are length and width of the second rectangle?

    a. 1.5 meters by 3 meters
    b. 3.5 meters by 6.5 meters
    c. 6 meters by 12 meters
    d. 1 meter by 2.5 meters

44. What is the volume of this rectangular prism?

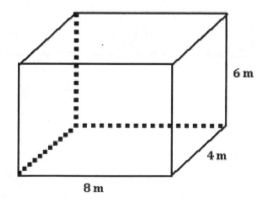

    a. 18 m³
    b. 192 m³
    c. 206 m³
    d. 186 m³

45. What is the measure of angle A?

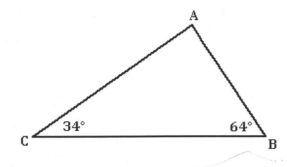

   a. 86°
   b. 82°
   c. 78°
   d. 92°

46. Elaine represents an equation using the algebra tiles shown below

Given that ⬜ **represents** x, ⬜ **represents positive 1, and** ⬛ **represents negative 1, which of the following represents the solution to the equation?**

   a. $x = -6$
   b. $x = 4$
   c. $x = 12$
   d. $x = -4$

47. A group of 500 7th grade students were surveyed, and the results are shown in the graph below. How many of the students preferred comedy movies?

Favorite Type of Movie

0%

   a. 180
   b. 200
   c. 220
   d. 240

19

48. The 7th grade students at Lincoln Junior High School were surveyed regarding the number of hours they spend playing video games each week. Data comparing boys and girls are summarized on the box-and-whisker plots below. Which of the following statements is true?

Number of Hours Spent Playing Video Games Each Week

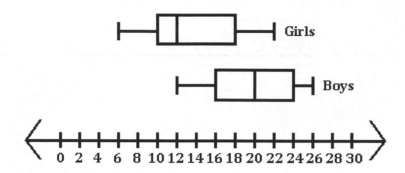

a. The greatest number of hours played by the boys is 24 hours.
b. The least number of hours played by the girls is ten hours.
c. The median number of hours played by boys is eight more than the median number of hours played by girls.
d. More than half of the girls play less than the median number of hours.

49. Aubrey planted fruit trees on her farm. The number of each type of tree planted is shown in the table below.

Type of Tree	Number of Trees
Apple Tree	8
Peach Tree	18
Fig Tree	12
Pear Tree	3

Which circle graph represents the percentage of each type of tree planted?

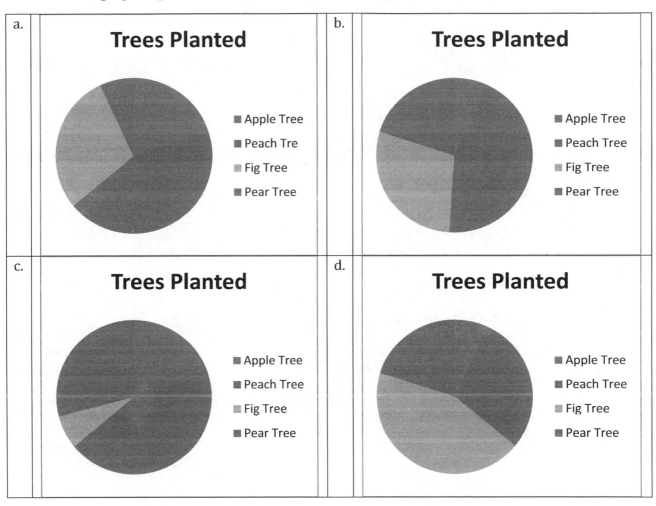

50. Diane Miller earned $32,000 this year in taxable income. If she must pay a federal income tax of 18.5%, how much income tax must she pay?

    a. $6,400
    b. $592,000
    c. $5,760
    d. $5,920

51. Bill Porter plans a budget based on his yearly net income of $48,000. What percent of his income has he budgeted for retirement savings?

Expense	Amount
Housing	$12,000
Food	$9,600
Utilities	$7,200
Retirement Savings	$6,240
Emergency Savings	$4,800
Car	$4,800
Other	$3,360

    a. 7%
    b. 25%
    c. 15%
    d. 13%

52. Scott Tillman is researching buying a new washing machine. Which of the following incentives provides the largest discount?

    a. A 15% coupon applied to a purchase price of $399.99
    b. A 35% rebate applied to a purchase price of $424.99
    c. A 20% coupon applied to a purchase price of $403.99
    d. A 40% rebate applied to a purchase price of $299.99

53. Mrs. Thurman has checked several stores to find the best deal on a new refrigerator. Which of the following options provides the lowest cost?

    a. A 20% rebate applied to a purchase price of $1,850
    b. A 25% rebate applied to a purchase price of $2,250
    c. A 10% coupon applied to a purchase price of $1,725
    d. A 35% coupon applied to a purchase price of $3,250

54. Mia estimates her yearly budget to be $37,440. If she works 40 hours per week, what is the minimum hourly wage she needs to earn to meet her financial needs?

    a. $22
    b. $16
    c. $20
    d. $18

- 52 -

Answer Key and Explanations for Math Test #1

TEKS Standard (7.4)(D)

1. D: In order to convert the given fraction to a percentage, divide 2 by 7. Doing so gives a decimal of approximately 0.29. The decimal can be converted to a percentage by multiplying by 100, which moves the decimal point two places to the right and gives 29%.

TEKS Standard (7.9)(A)

2. C: The square has an area of 16 square units, with 4 units comprising the length of each side. Therefore, the square root of the area is 4.

TEKS Standard (7.4)(D)

3. B: The following proportion can be written $\frac{4}{2} = \frac{x}{18}$. Solving for x gives $x = 36$. Thus, there are 36 data analysis problems on the test.

TEKS Standard (7.3)(B)

4. D: In order to determine the amount available to each guest, the total amount of prepared lemonade should be divided by 25 guests. Thus, the expression $2\frac{1}{2} \div 25$ represents the amount that each guest has available for consumption. The mixed fraction can be rewritten as $\frac{5}{2}$. The expression can be simplified by writing $\frac{5}{2} \div 25 = \frac{5}{2} \times \frac{1}{25}$, which equals $\frac{5}{50}$, or $\frac{1}{10}$.

TEKS Standard (7.3)(A)

5. D: The order of operations states that numbers with exponents must be evaluated first. Thus, the expression can be rewritten as $64 + 12 \div 4 + 64 \times 3$. Next, multiplication and division must be computed as they appear from left to right in the expression. Thus, the expression can be further simplified as $64 + 3 + 192$, which equals 259.

TEKS Standard (7.4)(D)

6. B: The discounted price is 25% less than the original price. Therefore, the discounted price can be written as $36.95 - ((0.25)(36.95))$, which equals approximately 27.71. Thus, the discounted price of the jacket is $27.71.

TEKS Standard (7.4)(D)

7. B: In order to find the percentage discount, the following equation can be written: $36,549.15 = 42,999 - 42,999x$. The equation can be solved by writing: $36,549.15 - 42,999 = -42,999x$, which simplifies to $-6,449.85 = -42,999x$, with $x = 0.15$; therefore, the percent discount is 15%.

TEKS Standard (7.4)(D)

8. B: In order to find the unit rate, the cost of the bottle should be divided by the number of fluid ounces contained in the bottle: $\frac{\$3.96}{20} \approx 0.20$. Thus, the cost per fluid ounce is approximately $0.20.

TEKS Standard (7.4)(D)

9. C: Since the lengths of Triangle B are related to the lengths of Triangle A by a scale factor of $\frac{1}{4}$, each side length of Triangle A should be multiplied by the factor $\frac{1}{4}$: $12 \times \frac{1}{4} = 3$; $8 \times \frac{1}{4} = 2$; $16 \times \frac{1}{4} = 4$. The side lengths of Triangle B measure 3 cm, 2 cm, and 4 cm, respectively.

TEKS Standard (7.4)(E)

10. B: One decimeter equals 10 centimeters, so the following proportion can be written: $\frac{1}{0.1} = \frac{x}{2.5}$. Solving for x gives $x = 25$. Thus, 2.5 decimeters is equal to 25 centimeters.

TEKS Standard (7.5)(A)

11. D: Based on the information given in the problem, for a sphere with a radius of 2 inches, the following equation can be written: $33.49 = 8\pi x$, where x represents the unknown ratio. Solving for x gives $x = \frac{4}{3}$. The ratio for a sphere with a radius of 4 inches can be determined using the equation $267.95 = 64\pi x$. Again, the ratio equals $\frac{4}{3}$. A check of each of the spheres shows the ratio to be $\frac{4}{3}$.

TEKS Standard (7.7)(A)

12. C: The equation that represents the relationship between the position number, n, and the value of the term, a_n, is $a_n = -3n + 8$. Notice each n is multiplied by –3, with 8 added to that value. Substituting position number 1 for n gives $a_n = -3(1) + 8$, which equals 5. Substitution of the remaining position numbers does not provide a counterexample to this procedure.

TEKS Standard (7.10)(A)

13. B: The algebra tiles represent the equation $x + 6 = 15$. Solving for x gives $x = 9$. Note that 6 unit squares are removed from each side of the equation to reveal the remaining 9 unit squares equivalent to the variable x.

TEKS Standard (7.10)(A)

14. D: The constant amount Kevin pays is $12.95; this amount represents the y-intercept. The variable amount is represented by the expression $0.07x$, where x represents the number of text messages sent and $0.07 represents the constant rate of change or slope. Thus, his total cost can be represented by the equation $y = \$0.07x + \$12.95$.

TEKS Standard (7.3)(A)

15. C: The cost per box can be determined by dividing the total cost, c, by the number of boxes, b, included in each total cost. Thus, the cost per box, x, can be determined by dividing c by b. Notice that $15.00 divided by 4 equals a rate of $3.75 per box. A check of the cost per box for the remaining number of boxes confirms a rate of $3.75 per box.

TEKS Standard (7.7)(A)

16. A: The plotted point has an x-value of –2 and a y-value of 5. Thus, the point can be written as an ordered pair in the form (–2, 5).

17. C: The circumference of a circle can be determined by using the formula $C = \pi d$. A radius of 23 cm indicates a diameter of 46 cm, or twice that length. Substitution of 46 cm for d and 3.14 for π gives the following: $C = 3.14 \cdot 46$, which equals 144.44. Thus, the circumference of the circle is approximately 144.44 cm.

TEKS Standard (7.9)(A)

18. D: The B in the formula $V = Bh$ represents the area of the triangular base. The formula for the area of a triangle is $\frac{1}{2}bh$, where b represents the length of the triangle's base and h represents the triangle's height.

TEKS Standard (7.9)(A)

19. A: The dimensions of the rectangular prism can be rounded to 14 cm, 9 cm, and 12 cm. The volume of a rectangular prism can be determined by finding the product of the length, width, and height. Therefore, the volume is approximately equal to $14 \times 9 \times 12$, or $1{,}512$ cm^3.

TEKS Standard (7.9)(A)

20. C: The volume of a cylindrical can be found using the formula $V = \pi r^2 h$, where r represents the radius and h represents the height. Substitution of the given radius and height gives $V = \pi(3.5)^2 \cdot 8$, which is approximately 307.72. Thus, the volume of the can is approximately 307.72 cm^3.

TEKS Standard (7.9)(A)

21. C: The volume of a triangular prism can be determined using the formula $V = \frac{1}{2}bhl$, where b represents the length of the base of each triangular face, h represents the height of each triangular face, and l represents the length of the prism. Substitution of the given values into the formula gives $V = \frac{1}{2} \cdot 4 \cdot 7 \cdot 11$, which equals 154. Thus, the volume of the candy box is 154 cubic inches.

TEKS Standard (7.6)(A)

22. C: The sample space of independent events is equal to the product of the sample space of each event. The sample space of rolling a die is 6; the sample space of spinning a spinner with four equal sections is 4. Therefore, the overall sample space is equal to 6×4, or 24.

TEKS Standard (7.6)(A)

23. B: Flipping a coin three times has the following possible outcomes: HHH, HTH, THT, TTT, HHT, TTH, HTT, and THH. Since there are 8 possible outcomes, the sample space is 8.

TEKS Standard (7.6)(D)

24. A: The events are independent since Sarah replaces the first die. The probability of two independent events can be found using the formula $P(A \text{ and } B) = P(A) \cdot P(B)$. The probability of pulling out a blue die is $\frac{2}{12}$. The probability of pulling out a green die is $\frac{4}{12}$. The probability of pulling out a blue die and a green die is $\frac{2}{12} \cdot \frac{4}{12}$, which simplifies to $\frac{1}{18}$.

TEKS Standard (7.12)(C)

25. C: The score that has approximately 50% above and 50% below is approximately 500 (517 to be exact). The scores can be manually written by choosing either the lower or upper end of each interval and using the frequency to determine the number of times to record each score, i.e., using the lower end of each interval shows an approximate value of 465 for the median; using the upper end of each interval shows an approximate value of 530 for the median. A score of 500 (and the exact median of 517) is found between 465 and 530.

TEKS Standard (7.6)(C)

26. C: The average age indicates the mean. The mean is calculated by summing all ages and dividing by the number of dogs in the sample. Thus, the mean can be calculated by writing $\frac{6+7+2+8+4+1+7+8+3+1+8+2}{12}$, which equals 4.75.

TEKS Standard (7.6)(D)

27. A: The probability of getting an even number is $\frac{3}{6}$. The probability of getting heads is $\frac{1}{2}$. The probability of both events occurring can be calculated by multiplying the probabilities of the individual events: $\frac{3}{6} \cdot \frac{1}{2}$ equals $\frac{1}{4}$.

TEKS Standard (7.2)(A)

28. A: Natural numbers are a subset of whole numbers. Integers are a subset of rational numbers. Whole numbers are a subset of integers and rational numbers. Therefore, choice A is correct.

TEKS Standard (7.6)(A)

29. A: The probability of a simple event is the ratio of the number of favorable outcomes to the number of possible outcomes. Favorable outcomes include 1, 2, 3, and 4. Possible outcomes include 1, 2, 3, 4, 5, and 6. The $P(< 5) = \frac{4}{6}$, which reduces to $\frac{2}{3}$. Therefore, choice A is correct.

TEKS Standard (7.6)(E)

30. A: The jar only holds red and green marbles. If the event is "drawing a red marble," then the complement of the event is "drawing a green marble." The probability of the complement of an event is the difference of 1 and the probability of the event. Then *P(green) = 1 – P(red)* or *P(green) =* $1 - \frac{7}{12} = \frac{12}{12} - \frac{7}{12} = \frac{5}{12}$. Therefore, choice A is correct.

TEKS Standard (7.6)(I)

31. B: The total number of students surveyed was 48 + 32 + 20 + 12 + 8 or 120. Only 20 of those students chose sausage pizza. The probability that a student prefers sausage is $\frac{20}{120}$, or $\frac{1}{6}$. Therefore, choice B is correct.

TEKS Standard (7.4)(C)

32. C: The constant of proportionality, *k*, is determined by $k = \frac{y}{x}$. Then $k = \frac{8.50}{1}$, or 8.50. Therefore, choice C is correct.

TEKS Standard (7.10)(B)

33. D: First, subtract 5 from both sides of the inequality, which yields $-2x > 8$. Then, divide both sides by -2. Remember to reverse the symbol since the inequality is being divided by a negative number. This yields $x < -4$, which is graphed on a number line with an open circle at -4 and shading to the left. Therefore, choice D is correct.

TEKS Standard (7.10)(A)

34. B: The total cost of the soda and pizza must be less than or equal to $50. Since each pizza cost $8, $8n$ represents the cost of n pizzas, and since Steven plans to spend $10 on soda, $8n + 10$ represents the cost of the pizza and soda together, which must be less than or equal to $50. The correct inequality is $8n + 10 \leq 50$. Therefore, choice B is correct.

TEKS Standard (7.10)(C)

35. B: Let x represent the amount of money saved, $52 the amount earned mowing yards, and $14 the amount spent on a birthday present. Then $52 – $14 = x. This can be rearranged as

$14 + x = 52$. Therefore, choice B is correct. 2.7.10

TEKS Standard (7.11)(A)

36. C: Subtracting 320 from both sides yields $-12m = -240$. Dividing both sides by -12 yields $m = 20$. Therefore, choice C is correct.

TEKS Standard (7.11)(B)

37. D: This problem can be solved by substituting each option into the inequality: substituting $b = 12$ results in $(30)(12) < 372$, or $360 < 272$, which is a true statement. Alternatively, solve the inequality for b by dividing both sides by 30, which yields $b < 12.4$; of the choices, only 12 is less than 12.4. Therefore, choice D is correct.

TEKS Standard (7.11)(A)

38. B: The first step in solving $-2 - 3x = -14$ is to add 2 to both sides. This results in $-3x = -12$. Dividing both sides by -3 yields $x = 4$. Therefore, choice B is correct.

TEKS Standard (7.4)(E)

39. A: When setting up a proportion, it's important to remember that like quantities must be placed in the numerators, and like quantities must be placed in the denominators. The general idea for a problem like this is $\frac{\text{feet}}{\text{miles}} = \frac{\text{feet}}{\text{miles}}$. The correct proportion is $\frac{5,280}{1} = \frac{26,400}{x}$. Therefore, choice A is correct.

TEKS Standard (7.5)(C)

40. C: The corresponding sides of similar triangles are proportional. In these triangles, RQ corresponds to UT, QS corresponds to TV, and RS corresponds to UV. Therefore, $\frac{QS}{RS} = \frac{TV}{UV}$.

Choice C is correct.

TEKS Standard (7.5)(B)

41. C: The ratio of the circumference of a circle to the diameter of the circle is pi. This can be written as $\frac{C}{d} = \pi$. Therefore, choice C is correct.

TEKS Standard (7.5)(C)

42. B: Since $\triangle ABE$ and $\triangle ACD$ have two congruent angles (notice that both triangles have $\angle A$ in common, and $\angle B \cong \angle C$ since both angles measure 70°), their third angles must also be congruent. Thus, $\triangle ABE$ is similar to $\triangle ACD$. Since the corresponding sides of similar triangles are proportional, $\frac{AB}{AC} = \frac{AE}{AD}$. However, the lengths BE and CD are not equal. Therefore, choice B is correct.

TEKS Standard (7.5)(A)

43. A: Since the scale factor is less than 1, the second rectangle is smaller than the first rectangle. To find the dimensions of the second rectangle, multiply each dimension of the first rectangle by $\frac{1}{2}$ or 0.5. Since (0.5)(3) is 1.5, and (0.5)(6) is 3, the dimensions of the second rectangle are 1.5 meters by 3 meters. Therefore, choice A is correct.

TEKS Standard (7.9)(A)

44. B: The volume of the rectangular prism is found by multiplying the area of the base times the height, or Volume = length × width × height. So, $V = (8m)(4m)(6m) = 192$ m^3. Therefore, choice B is correct.

TEKS Standard (7.11)(C)

45. B: The sum of the angles of a triangle is 180°. The measure of angle A can be found by 180°− (34° + 64°), or 180°− 98°, which is 82°. Therefore, choice B is correct.

TEKS Standard (7.11)(A)

46. B: The equation represented by the algebra tiles is $3x - 8 = 4$. Solving for x gives $3x = 12$, so $x = 4$. The equation can be visually solved by adding 8 green tiles to each side, and using the additive inverse property to isolate the $3x$. The equation can then be written as $3x = 12$. Each x can be mapped to 4 positive integer tiles. Thus, $x = 4$.

TEKS Standard (7.6)(G)

47. B: To determine the number of students that preferred comedy movies, find 40% of 500. Multiplying (0.40)(500) yields 200. Therefore, choice B is correct.

TEKS Standard (7.12)(A)

48. C: The median is the same as Quartile 2. The median for the girls is twelve hours. The median for the boys is twenty hours. The median number of hours played by boys is eight more than the median number of hours played by girls. Therefore, choice C is correct.

TEKS Standard (7.12)(B)

49. A: The percentages of each type of tree are as follows: Apple tree – 20%; Peach tree – 44%; Fig tree – 29%, and Pear tree – 7%. The circle graph for Choice A accurately represents these percentages.

TEKS Standard (7.13)(A)

50. D: To determine the federal income tax, find 18.5% of $32,000. Multiplying (0.185)($32,000) yields $5,920. Therefore, choice D is correct.

TEKS Standard (7.13)(B)

51. D: The question asks, "What percent of $48,000 is $6,240?" Dividing $6,240 by $48,000 yields 0.13. Converting the decimal 0.13 to a percent yields 13%. Therefore, choice D is correct.

TEKS Standard (7.13)(F)

52. B: The discount for choice A is (0.15)($399.99), or $60.00. The discount for choice B is (0.35)($424.99), or $148.75. The discount for choice C is (0.20)($403.99), or $80.80. The discount for choice D is (0.40)($299.99), or $120.00. Therefore, choice B is correct.

TEKS Standard (7.13)(F)

53. A: The refrigerator in choice A costs $1,850– (0.20)($1,850), or $1,480. The refrigerator in choice B costs $2,250– (0.25)($2,250), or $1,687.50. The refrigerator in choice C costs 1,725– (0.10)(1,725), or $1,552.50. The refrigerator in choice D costs $3,250– (0.35)($3,250), or $2,112.5. Therefore, choice A is correct.

TEKS Standard (7.13)(D)

54. D: The minimum weekly wage needed is found by dividing $37,440 by 52 weeks in a year, which results in $720. The minimum hourly wage is found by dividing $720 by 40 hours per week, which results in $18 per hour. Therefore, choice D is correct.

Mathematics Practice Test #2

1. Amanda has finished 80% of a grant proposal. Which of the following fractions represents the amount she has finished?

    a. $\dfrac{3}{4}$

    b. $\dfrac{7}{9}$

    c. $\dfrac{4}{5}$

    d. $\dfrac{6}{7}$

2. According to the order of operations, which of the following steps should be completed immediately following the evaluation of the squared number when evaluating the expression

$$9 - 18^2 \times 2 + 12 \div 4$$

    a. Subtract 18^2 from 9
    b. Multiply the squared value by 2
    c. Divide 12 by 4
    d. Add 2 and 12

3. A publishing company has been given 29 manuscripts to review. If the company divides the work equally amongst 8 editors, which of the following represents the number of manuscript each editor will review?

    a. $3\dfrac{3}{5}$

    b. $3\dfrac{5}{8}$

    c. $3\dfrac{7}{9}$

    d. $3\dfrac{2}{3}$

4. Given the counters shown below, where  represents negative 1 and ⬤ represents positive 1, what is the sum?

    a. −20
    b. 4
    c. 20
    d. −4

5. Which of the following is equivalent to $-8^2 + (17 - 9) \times 4 + 7$?

    a. −217
    b. 24
    c. −64
    d. −25

6. Jason chooses a number that is the square root of four less than two times Amy's number. If Amy's number is 20, what is Jason's number?

    a. 6
    b. 7
    c. 8
    d. 9

7. Robert secures three new clients every eight months. After how many months has he secured 24 new clients?

    a. 64
    b. 58
    c. 52
    d. 66

8. A house is priced at $278,000. The price of the house has been reduced by $12,600. Which of the following best represents the percentage of the reduction?

    a. 3%
    b. 4%
    c. 5%
    d. 6%

9. A 20-ounce drink costs $1.19. Which of the following best represents the cost per ounce?

    a. $0.07
    b. $0.06
    c. $0.04
    d. $0.08

10. Mel studied 25 hours per week when he took four college courses. If he spends the same amount of time studying per course, how many hours will he spend studying when he takes five college courses?

    a. 30.75
    b. 32.50
    c. 31.75
    d. 31.25

11. Eric sprints a distance of 42 meters. How many inches does he sprint? Use the approximation **1 m ≈ 1 yd**.

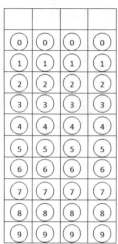

12. A cone has a radius of 4 cm and an approximate volume of 150.72 cm³. What is the height of the cone?

    a. 7 cm
    b. 9 cm
    c. 8 cm
    d. 12 cm

13. What is the 19th term in the sequence $-10, -7, -4, -1, 2, ...$?

14. Which of the following formulas represents the value of the nth term as 4 less than 6 times the position of the nth term?

    a. $a_n = 4n - 6$
    b. $a_n = 6n + 4$
    c. $a_n = 6n - 4$
    d. $a_n = n - 10$

15. The 12th term in a sequence with a common difference of −9 is −106. Which of the following formulas can be used to represent this sequence?

    a. $y = -9x + 4$
    b. $y = -9x - 6$
    c. $y = -9x + 2$
    d. $y = -9x - 8$

16. A round trip airline ticket costs $406. The airline Aidan is using charges $35 per checked bag. Which of the following equations represents the total cost for the ticket and checked bag(s)?

    a. $y = 35 + 406x$
    b. $y = 441x$
    c. $y = \frac{406}{35}x$
    d. $y = 406 + 35x$

17. Which of the following describes *all* requirements of similar polygons?

    a. Similar polygons have congruent corresponding angles and proportional corresponding sides
    b. Similar polygons have congruent corresponding angles and congruent corresponding sides
    c. Similar polygons have proportional corresponding sides
    d. Similar polygons have congruent corresponding angles

18. Marlo needs to build a right triangular brace with an area greater than 49 square inches but less than 52 square inches. Which dimensions should she use for the base and height of the brace?

    a. 6 inches and 18 inches
    b. 13 inches and 8 inches
    c. 11 inches and 9 inches
    d. 7 inches and 14 inches

19. The volume of a cylinder is equal to the product of the area of one base and the height. Which of the following represents the area of one of the bases?

    a. πr
    b. πd
    c. πd^2
    d. πr^2

20. Judith purchased a box from the U.S. Postal Service with dimensions of 12 inches by 8 inches by 6 inches. How many cubic inches of space inside the box does she have available for use?

⓪	⓪	⓪
①	①	①
②	②	②
③	③	③
④	④	④
⑤	⑤	⑤
⑥	⑥	⑥
⑦	⑦	⑦
⑧	⑧	⑧
⑨	⑨	⑨

21. A cylindrical post has a height of 12 feet and a diameter of 8 inches. Which of the following best represents the volume of the post?

    a. 6.87 ft^3
    b. 8.72 ft^3
    c. 4.19 ft^3
    d. 12.56 ft^3

22 A pothole has a radius of 9 inches. Which of the following best represents the distance around the pothole?

    a. 14.13 inches
    b. 28.26 inches
    c. 42.39 inches
    d. 56.52 inches

23. What is the sample space when rolling two standard dice?

    a. 18
    b. 6
    c. 12
    d. 36

24. What is the sample space when flipping a coin 9 times?

    a. 256
    b. 4,096
    c. 512
    d. 1,028

25. Kevin spins a spinner with 8 sections labeled 1 through 8. He also flips a coin. What is the probability he will land on a number less than 5 and get tails?

    a. $\dfrac{7}{8}$

    b. $\dfrac{1}{4}$

    c. $\dfrac{5}{16}$

    d. $\dfrac{1}{2}$

26. A box contains 8 yellow marbles, 9 orange marbles, and 1 green marble. What is the probability that Ann pulls out a yellow marble, replaces it, and then pulls a green marble?

    a. $\dfrac{4}{153}$

    b. $\dfrac{1}{2}$

    c. $\dfrac{4}{9}$

    d. $\dfrac{2}{81}$

27. Chandler wishes to examine the median house value in his new hometown. Which graphical representation will most clearly indicate the median?

    a. Box-and-whisker plot
    b. Stem-and-leaf plot
    c. Line plot
    d. Bar graph

28. The number of long distance minutes Amanda used per week for business purposes is shown in the table below. What is the median number of long-distance minutes she used?

Week	Number of Minutes
1	289
2	255
3	322
4	291
5	306
6	302
7	411
8	418

0	0	0
1	1	1
2	2	2
3	3	3
4	4	4
5	5	5
6	6	6
7	7	7
8	8	8
9	9	9

- 65 -

29. A university reported the number of incoming freshmen from 2002 to 2011. The data is shown in the table below.

Year	Number of Incoming Freshmen
2002	7,046
2003	7,412
2004	6,938
2005	7,017
2006	7,692
2007	8,784
2008	7,929
2009	7,086
2010	8,017
2011	8,225

Based on the 10-year sample of data, which of the following represents the approximate average number of incoming freshmen?

    a. 7,618
    b. 7,615
    c. 7,621
    d. 7,624

30. Which of the following is the correct sample space for tossing a coin and rolling a six-sided die?

    a. {H1, H2, H3, T4, T5, T6}
    b. {H1, H3, H5, T2, T4, T6}
    c. {HH, HT, TH, TT, 1, 2, 3, 4, 5, 6}
    d. {H1, H2, H3, H4, H5, H6, T1, T2, T3, T4, T5, T6}

31. A student tosses two coins at the same time. What is the probability of tossing two heads?

    a. $\dfrac{1}{2}$
    b. $\dfrac{2}{3}$
    c. $\dfrac{1}{4}$
    d. $\dfrac{1}{3}$

32. A student tosses a coin ten times and records her results in the table below. Which of the following statements is true?

Toss 1	Toss 2	Toss3	Toss4	Toss 5	Toss 6	Toss 7	Toss8	Toss 9	Toss 10
Tails	Tails	Heads	Heads	Tails	Tails	Tails	Heads	Tails	Heads

    a. The experimental probability of tossing heads is equal to the theoretical probability of tossing heads.

    b. The theoretical probability of tossing heads is $\dfrac{3}{5}$.

    c. The experimental probability of tossing heads is $\dfrac{1}{2}$.

    d. The experimental probability of tossing heads is less than the theoretical probability of tossing heads.

33. A six-sided die is rolled five times. If the first four rolls are all even numbers, what is the probability of the fifth roll being an even number?

a. $\frac{2}{3}$

b. $\frac{5}{6}$

c. $\frac{1}{2}$

d. $\frac{1}{6}$

34. The cost of tickets to a community event is shown in the table below. Which of the following is the unit rate?

Number of tickets	5	10	20	30
Cost ($)	30	60	120	180

a. $\frac{6}{1}$

b. $\frac{1}{6}$

c. $\frac{5}{1}$

d. $\frac{1}{5}$

35. The length of a baby python changes from 15 to 18 centimeters. Which of the following is the percent change to the nearest whole percent?

a. 17% increase

b. 20% increase

c. 17% decrease

d. 20% decrease

36. A truck travels 220 miles on ten gallons of gas. How many gallons of gas are needed for the truck to travel 330 miles?

a. 20

b. 17

c. 12

d. 15

37. The cost of pineapples is represented by the equation $C = 4.50n$, in which n is the number of pineapples and C is the cost in dollars. Which of the following tables represents this linear relationship?

a.

n	0	2	4	6
C	0	9.00	18.00	27.00

b.

n	1	3	5	7
C	0	9.00	18.00	27.00

c.

n	0	2	4	6
C	4.50	9.00	18.00	27.00

d.

n	1	2	3	4
C	4.50	9.00	18.00	27.00

38. Which of the following equations represents the linear relationship shown by the table below?

Time (Hours), x	Distance (Miles), y
0	0
2	70
3	105
4	140
5	175

a. $y = 140x + 35$
b. $y = 35x + 70$
c. $y = 35x$
d. $y = 70x$

39. Which of the following is the solution to the equation $200 + 25m = 350$?

a. 6
b. 8
c. 14
d. 22

40. Which of the following sets is the solution set for $4m - 1 < -12$ if the replacement set is {-6, -4, -3, -2, 0, 5}?

a. {-6, -4, -3, -2}
b. {-2, 0, 5}
c. {-6, -4}
d. {-6, -4, -3}

- 68 -

41. Which of the following sets is the solution set for $-4 + 6s = 20$ if the replacement set is {-4, -2, -1, 0, 1, 4, 6}?

    a. {0, 4}
    b. {-4}
    c. {4}
    d. {1}

42. If 1 mile = 5,280 feet, which of the following proportions can be used to determine the number of miles equal to 26,400 feet?

    a. $\dfrac{5{,}280}{1} = \dfrac{26{,}400}{x}$

    b. $\dfrac{5{,}280}{1} = \dfrac{x}{26{,}400}$

    c. $\dfrac{5{,}280}{x} = \dfrac{26{,}400}{1}$

    d. $\dfrac{5{,}280}{26{,}400} = \dfrac{x}{1}$

43. If 1 inch = 2.54 cm, how many centimeters are there in 5 feet?

    a. 132.8 cm
    b. 164.6 cm
    c. 148.6 cm
    d. 152.4 cm

44. Which of the following statements is true?

    a. All triangles are similar.
    b. All trapezoids are similar.
    c. All polygons are similar.
    d. All squares are similar.

45. This pair of polygons is similar. Find x.

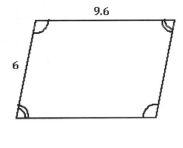

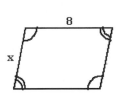

    a. 5.4
    b. 5
    c. 4
    d. 4.8

- 69 -

46. A tree casts a shadow that is 4 feet long. At the same time, a 5-foot girl standing next to the tree casts a shadow that is 2.5 feet long. Which of the following proportions can be used to determine the height of the tree?

a. $\dfrac{x}{4} = \dfrac{5}{2.5}$

b. $\dfrac{x}{4} = \dfrac{2.5}{5}$

c. $\dfrac{x}{2.5} = \dfrac{4}{2.5}$

d. $\dfrac{x}{4} = \dfrac{2.5}{5}$

47. A light pole casts a shadow that is 6 feet long. At the same time, a 4-foot decorative tree next to the light pole casts a shadow that is 1.6 feet long. What is the height of the light pole?

a. 15 feet
b. 12 feet
c. 18 feet
d. 10 feet

48. What is the scale factor needed to dilate this preimage to this image?

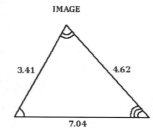

a. 1.4
b. 0.8
c. 2.1
d. 1.1

49. The bar graph shows the number of years that each of four 7th graders has been taking violin lessons. Which student has been taking lessons the longest?

Playing Violin

a. Reese
b. Daphnia
c. Nathan
d. Connor

50. Mr. Estes purchases a car priced at $18,500. If the sales tax is 7%, what is the total cost of the car?

a. $19,795
b. $129,500
c. $20, 125
d. $19, 495

51. Johnny Vera earns $3,200 during the summer working for a local farmer. If he budgets 7% of his income for gas expenses, how much of his summer income has he budgeted for gas?

a. $224
b. $248
c. $263
d. $288

52. Which of the following statements correctly compares the simple interest earned on $10,000 for three years at 7% and the interest earned on the same principal at the same rate if compounded annually?

a. The compound interest earned of $2550.43 is $150.43 more than the simple interest earned of $2,100.
b. The compound interest earned of $2555.43 is $155.43 more than the simple interest earned of $2,100.
c. The compound interest earned of $2350.43 is $150.43 more than the simple interest earned of $2,200.
d. The compound interest earned of $2355.43 is $155.43 more than the simple interest earned of $2,200.

53. Stanley earns an average of $72 per month doing odd jobs for a neighbor. He budgets 30% for college savings. How much does he budget each month for college savings?

    a. $27.40
    b. $25.30
    c. $21.60
    d. $23.90

54. Tim Taylor earns $225 per month working at a veterinary clinic. He budgets $125 per month for college savings. Approximately what percent of his income has Tim budgeted towards college savings?

    a. 45%
    b. 48%
    c. 56%
    d. 59%

Answer Key and Explanations for Math Test #2

TEKS Standard (7.4)(D)

1. C: The fraction $\frac{4}{5}$ can be converted to a decimal by dividing 4 by 5. Doing so gives 0.80, which is equal to 80%.

TEKS Standard (7.3)(B)

2. B: The order of operations states that multiplication and division, as they appear from left to right in the expression, should be completed following the evaluation of exponents. Therefore, after evaluating the squared number, that value should be multiplied by 2.

TEKS Standard (7.3)(A)

3. B: In order to determine the number of manuscripts each editor will review, the total number of manuscripts should be divided by the number of editors; $29 \div 8$ can be written as $\frac{29}{8}$, which simplifies to the mixed fraction $3\frac{5}{8}$. Notice that the quotient is 3 with a remainder of 5.

TEKS Standard (7.3)(A)

4. D: The counters represent the expression $-12 + 8$, which equals -4. Using the additive inverse property, the eight negative 1 integers and eight positive 1 integers cancel one another, leaving four negative 1 integers, written as -4.

TEKS Standard (7.3)(B)

5. D: The order of operations requires evaluation of the expression inside the parentheses as a first step. Thus, the expression can be re-written as $-8^2 + 8 \times 4 + 7$. Next, the integer with the exponent must be evaluated. Doing so gives $-64 + 8 \times 4 + 7$. The order of operations next requires all multiplications and divisions to be computed as they appear from left to right. Thus, the expression can be written as $-64 + 32 + 7$. Finally, the addition may be computed as it appears from left to right. The expression simplifies to $-32 + 7$, or -25.

TEKS Standard (7.10)(C)

6. A: Jason's number can be determined by writing the following expression: $\sqrt{2x - 4}$, where x represents Amy's number. Substitution of 20 for x gives $\sqrt{2(20) - 4}$, which simplifies to $\sqrt{36}$, or 6. Thus, Jason's number is 6. Jason's number can also be determined by working backwards. If Jason's number is the square root of 4 less than 2 times Amy's number, Amy's number should first be multiplied by 2 with 4 subtracted from that product and the square root taken of the resulting difference.

TEKS Standard (7.4)(D)

7. A: The following proportion can be used to solve the problem: $\frac{3}{8} = \frac{24}{x}$. Solving for x gives: $3x = 192$, which simplifies to $x = 64$.

TEKS Standard (7.11)(A)

8. B: The original price was $290,600 ($278,000 + $12,600). In order to determine the percentage of reduction, the following equation can be written: $12,600 = \$290,600x$, which simplifies to $x \approx 0.04$, or 4%. Thus, the percentage of reduction was approximately 4%.

TEKS Standard (7.4)(B)

9. B: In order to find the unit rate, the cost of the drink should be divided by the number of ounces the drink contains: $\frac{\$1.19}{20} \approx 0.06$. Thus, the cost per ounce is approximately $0.06.

TEKS Standard (7.4)(D)

10. D: A proportion can be written to compare the number of hours spent studying for four courses to the number of hours spent studying for five courses. The following proportion can be written: $\frac{25}{4} = \frac{x}{5}$. Solving for x gives $x = 31.25$. Thus, Mel will spend 31.25 hours studying for 5 college courses.

TEKS Standard (7.4)(E)

11. 1,512: One foot contains 12 inches, and one meter contains approximately 3 feet. Thus, there are 36 inches in one meter; 42 meters contains 36×42 inches, or 1,512 inches.

TEKS Standard (7.9)(A)

12. B: The volume of a cone can be determined by using the formula $V = \frac{1}{3}\pi r^2 h$. Substitution of the radius and volume into the formula gives $150.72 = \frac{1}{3}\pi(4)^2 h$, which simplifies to $150.72 = \frac{1}{3}\pi 16h$. Division of each side of the equation by $\frac{1}{3}\pi 16$ gives $h = 9$. Thus, the height of the cone is 9 cm.

TEKS Standard §(7.10)(A)

13. 44: The sequence has a common difference of 3, so the slope is 3. The equation for finding the nth term of the sequence can thus be written as $y = 3x + b$. Substitution of the position number for x and the value of the nth term for y will reveal the y-intercept, or b. Using the first term, the following equation can be written $-10 = 3(1) + b$. Solving for b gives $b = -13$. The equation for finding the nth term can be written as $y = 3x - 13$. In order to find the 19th term, 19 should be substituted for x. Doing so gives $y = 3(19) - 13$, which equals 44. Thus, the 19th term is 44.

TEKS Standard (7.10)(A)

14. C: Translation of the value of the nth term indicates the value will be 4 less than 6 times the position of the number, or n. The expression "6 times n" is written as 6n; subtraction of 4 from this expression gives $6n - 4$. Thus, the value of the nth term, or a_n, is written as $a_n = 6n - 4$.

TEKS Standard (7.10)(A)

15. C: Evaluation of the formula $y = -9x + 2$ for an x-value of 12 gives a y-value of -106, the value of the 12th term. Thus, the formula given for Choice C can be used to represent the sequence.

TEKS Standard (7.10)(A)

16. D: The total cost y includes the constant price of the airline ticket plus the price of the baggage, which varies depending on the number of checked bags. The total cost y can be represented by the equation $y = 406 + 35x$, where x represents the number of checked bags

TEKS Standard (7.9)(A)

17. A: Similar polygons must have congruent corresponding angles and proportional corresponding sides. Both requirements must be fulfilled in order to declare similarity in polygons.

TEKS Standard (7.4)(C)

18. C: A triangle with a base of 11 inches and a height of 9 inches has an area equal to 1/2 (11)(9), or 49.5; an area of 49.5 square inches is greater than 49 square inches but less than 52 square inches. Therefore, she should use the dimensions of 11 inches and 9 inches.

TEKS Standard (7.9)(A)

19. D: The volume of a cylinder can be determined by using the following formula: $V = Bh$, where B represents the area of the base and h represents the height. The area of one of the bases refers to the area of one of the circular bases. The area of a circle is determined by πr^2; thus, the area of one of the cylindrical bases is represented by πr^2.

TEKS Standard (7.9)(A)

20. 576: The box is a rectangular prism, and the amount of available space inside the box is synonymous with the volume of the box. The volume of a rectangular prism is calculated by finding the product of the length, width, and height. Thus, the volume of the box is equal to 12 in × 8 in × 6 in, or 576 cubic inches.

TEKS Standard (7.9)(A)

21. C: The volume of a cylinder is determined by using the formula $V = \pi r^2 h$, where r represents the radius and h represents the height. The diameter is given in inches, whereas the height is given in feet. Thus, the radius of 4 inches must be converted to feet; 4 inches equals $\frac{1}{3}$ of a foot. The converted radius and given height can be substituted into the formula. Doing so gives: $V = \pi \left(\frac{1}{3}\right)^2 12$, which simplifies to $V = \pi \frac{1}{9}(12)$, which approximately equals 4.19 ft^3.

TEKS Standard (7.9)(B)

22. D: The distance around the pothole indicates the circumference of the pothole. The circumference of a circle can be determined by using the formula $C = \pi d$, where C represents the circumference and d represents the diameter. The diameter of the pothole is 18 inches (9 × 2). Substituting a diameter of 18 inches and 3.14 for the value of pi gives the following: $C = 3.14(18)$, or 56.52. Thus, the distance around the pothole is equal to 56.52 inches.

TEKS Standard (7.6)(A)

23. D: The sample space of rolling each die is 6. Thus, the sample space of rolling two dice is equal to the product of the sample spaces. 6 × 6 = 36; therefore, the sample space is equal to 36.

TEKS Standard (7.6)(A)

24. C: Flipping a coin one time has a sample space equal to 2, i.e., T or H. Flipping a coin 2 times has a sample space equal to 4, i.e., TT, HH, TH, HT. Flipping a coin 3 times has a sample space of 8, i.e., TTT, HHH, THT, HTH, TTH, HHT, THH, HTT. Notice that 2 is equal to 2^1, 4 is equal to 2^2, and 8 is equal to 2^3. The sample space of flipping a coin 9 times is equal to 2^9, or 512.

TEKS Standard (7.6)(D)

25. B: The events are independent since the spin of a spinner does not have an effect on the outcome of the flip of a coin. The probability of two independent events can be found using the formula $P(A \text{ and } B) = P(A) \cdot P(B)$. The probability of landing on a number less than 5 is $\frac{4}{8}$ since there are 4 possible numbers less than 5 (1, 2, 3, and 4). The probability of getting tails is $\frac{1}{2}$. The probability of landing on a number less than 5 and getting tails is $\frac{4}{8} \cdot \frac{1}{2}$, which equals $\frac{4}{16}$, or $\frac{1}{4}$.

TEKS Standard (7.6)(D)

26. D: The events are independent since Ann replaces the first marble drawn. The probability of two independent events can be found using the formula $P(A \text{ and } B) = P(A) \cdot P(B)$. The probability of pulling out a yellow marble is $\frac{8}{18}$. The probability of pulling out a green marble after the yellow marble has been replaced is $\frac{1}{18}$. The probability that Ann pulls out a yellow marble and then a green marble is $\frac{8}{18} \cdot \frac{1}{18}$, which equals $\frac{8}{324}$, which reduces to $\frac{2}{81}$.

TEKS Standard (7.12)(B)

27. A: The median can be determined using any of the given graphical representations. However, a box-and-whiskers plot actually includes a line drawn for the median, thus clearly indicating the value of the median.

TEKS Standard (7.12)(B)

28. 304: The median number of minutes can be determined by listing the number of minutes in order from least to greatest and calculating the average of the two middle values. The number of minutes can be written in ascending order as 255, 289, 291, 302, 306, 322, 411, and 418. The two middle values are 302 and 306. The average of these values can be determined by writing $\frac{302+306}{2}$, which equals 304. Thus, the median number of minutes is 304.

TEKS Standard (7.12)(B)

29. B: The average number (or mean) of incoming freshmen can be calculated by summing the numbers of incoming freshmen and dividing by the total number of years (or 10). Thus, the mean can be calculated by evaluating $\frac{76,146}{10}$, which equals 7,614.6. Since a fraction of a person cannot occur, the mean can be rounded to 7,615 freshmen.

TEKS Standard (7.6)(A)

30. D: A sample space shows all of the possible outcomes from tossing a coin and rolling a die. The toss of the coin can yield either heads (H) or tails (T). The roll of the die can yield 1, 2, 3, 4, 5, or 6. The sample space for this scenario is {H1, H2, H3, H4, H5, H6, T1, T2, T3, T4, T5, T6}. Therefore, choice D is correct.

31. C: This is an independent compound event. The probability for this event is equal to the product of the probabilities of each simple event involved. The probability of tossing heads for each coin is $\frac{1}{2}$. Thus, the probability of tossing heads for two coins at the same time is $\frac{1}{2} \cdot \frac{1}{2}$, which equals $\frac{1}{4}$. Therefore, choice C is correct.

32. D: The theoretical probability of tossing heads is always $\frac{1}{2}$. The experimental probability of tossing heads is determined from the data. The data shows that the student tosses heads four out of ten tosses. Accordingly, the experimental probability of tossing heads is $\frac{4}{10}$, or $\frac{2}{5}$. Since, $\frac{2}{5} < \frac{1}{2}$, the experimental probability of tossing heads is less than the theoretical probability of tossing heads. Therefore, choice D is correct. 1.7.6

33. C: The probability of the fifth roll is unaffected by the results of the first four rolls. The number of favorable outcomes is three. The number of possible outcomes is six. So, the probability of rolling an even number is $\frac{3}{6}$, or $\frac{1}{2}$. Therefore, choice C is correct.

34. A: The unit rate is determined by the ratio $\frac{\text{Cost(\$)}}{\text{Number of tickets}}$. Using the data from the first column from the table, the unit rate is $\frac{30}{5}$ or $\frac{6}{1}$. Therefore, choice A is correct.

35. B: Percent change is the ratio of amount of change to the original amount. This is an increase. The percent increase is determined by $\frac{18-15}{15} \times 100\%$, a 20% increase. Therefore, choice B is correct.

36. D: The truck travels 220 miles on ten gallons, which is $\frac{220 \text{ miles}}{10 \text{ gallons}}$ or $\frac{22 \text{ miles}}{1 \text{ gallon}}$. To find the number of gallons needed to travel 330 miles, divide 330 miles by $22 \frac{\text{miles}}{\text{gallon}}$. The truck needs 15 gallons. Therefore, choice D is correct.

37. A: The correct table can be determined by finding the table with a rate of change of 4.50. Using the first two columns of the table in choice A, the rate of change is equal to $\frac{9.00-0}{2-0}$, which is 4.50. Therefore, choice A is correct.

TEKS Standard (7.7)(A)

38. C: Since the relationship is linear, the equation is in the form of $y = mx + b$. The slope (m) is determined from the table by slope $= \frac{\text{change in } y \text{ (distance)}}{\text{change in } x \text{ (time)}}$. Using the second and third rows of the table yields slope $= \frac{105-70}{3-2}$, or 35. Since distance is 0 when time is 0, $b = 0$. The correct equation is $y = 35x$. Therefore, choice C is correct.

TEKS Standard (7.11)(A)

39. A: Subtracting 200 from both sides yields $200 - 200 + 25m = 350 - 200$, or $25m = 150$. Dividing both sides by 25 yields $m = 6$. Therefore, choice A is correct.

TEKS Standard (7.11)(B)

40. D: Since this is an inequality, there may be several members in the solution set. Each member of the replacement set is checked to determine if it makes the inequality a true statement. Only -6, -4, and -3 make this inequality a true statement. Therefore, choice D is correct.

TEKS Standard (7.11)(B)

41. C: Since this is a linear equation, the solution set can have only one member. Each member of the replacement set is substituted into the equation to see if the solution is the member of the solution set. Substituting in $s = 4$ makes $-4 + 6s = 20$ a true statement. The solution set is $\{4\}$. Therefore, choice C is correct.

TEKS Standard (7.4)(E)

42. A: When setting up a proportion, it's important to remember that like quantities must be placed in the numerators, and like quantities must be placed in the denominators. The general idea for a problem like this is $\frac{\text{feet}}{\text{miles}} = \frac{\text{feet}}{\text{miles}}$. The correct proportion is $\frac{5,280}{1} = \frac{26,400}{x}$. Therefore, choice A is correct.

TEKS Standard (7.4)(E)

43. D: This problem can be solved using unit rates and dimensional analysis like so: 5 feet x $\frac{12 \text{ inches}}{\text{foot}} \times \frac{2.54 \text{ cm}}{\text{inch}} = 152.4$ cm. Therefore, choice D is correct.

TEKS Standard (7.5)(A)

44. D: Similar figures have the same shape, and corresponding angles of the similar figures are congruent. Since all squares are quadrilaterals with four right angles and four congruent sides, all squares are similar. Not all triangles, trapezoids, or polygons are similar. Therefore, choice D is correct.

TEKS Standard (7.5)(A)

45. B: Since the polygons are similar, their corresponding sides are proportional. The length x can be determined by the proportion $\frac{x}{6} = \frac{8}{9.6}$. Finding cross products yields $9.6x = 48$. Dividing both sides by 9.6 shows that $x = 5$. Therefore, choice B is correct.

- 78 -

TEKS Standard (7.5)(C)

46. A: When setting up a proportion, like quantities need to be placed in the numerators and like quantities need to be placed in the denominators. For this problem, the proportion has the form of $\frac{object}{shadow} = \frac{object}{shadow}$. The proportion in the correct format is $\frac{x}{4} = \frac{5}{2.5}$. Therefore, choice A is correct.

TEKS Standard (7.5)(C)

47. A: A proportion can be written in the form of $\frac{object}{shadow} = \frac{object}{shadow}$. For this problem, the proportion is $\frac{x}{6} = \frac{4}{1.6}$. Cross multiplying yields $1.6x = 24$. Dividing the equation by 1.6 yields $x = 15$ feet. Therefore, choice A is correct.

TEKS Standard (7.5)(C)

48. D: Since the image is larger than the preimage, this is an enlargement with a scale factor that is greater than 1. Dividing the lengths of corresponding sides $\left(\frac{4.62}{4.20} = \frac{7.04}{6.40} = \frac{3.41}{3.10}\right)$ yields a scale factor of 1.1. Therefore, choice D is correct.

TEKS Standard (7.6)(G)

49. C: The height of the bar graph indicates the number of years each student has taken violin lessons. Since the bar representing Nathan's number of years is the tallest, Nathan has been taking lessons the longest. Therefore, choice C is correct.

TEKS Standard (7.13)(A)

50. A: The tax on the car is found by ($18,500)(0.07), or $1,295. The total price of the car is $18,500 + $1,295, or $19,795. Therefore, choice A is correct.

TEKS Standard (7.13)(B)

51. A: To find the amount of the summer income budgeted for gas, change the 7% to a decimal and multiply by the summer income: (0.07)($3,200). This yields $224. Therefore, choice A is correct.

TEKS Standard (7.13)(E)

52. A: The simple interest earned on $10,000 for three years at 7% is found by $i = (10,000)(0.07)(3) = \$2,100$. The interest earned if compounded annually can be calculated in steps. The interest earned for the first year is found by $i = (\$10,000)(0.07)(1) = \$700$. This interest is added to the principal, and interest earned for the second year is found by $i = (\$10,700)(0.07)(1) = \$749$. Again, this interest is added to the account, and the interest earned for the third year is found by $i = (\$11,449)(0.07)(1) = \$801.43$. The total interest earned over the three years is $700 + $749 + $801.43 = $2,550.43. The compound interest earned of $2,550.53 is $150.43 more than the simple interest earned of $2,100. Therefore, choice A is correct.

TEKS Standard (7.13)(D)

53. C: The amount he budgets for college savings is 30% of $72. Multiplying (0.30)($72) yields $21.60. Therefore, choice C is correct.

54. C: The percent budgeted towards college savings is determined by dividing $125 by $225 and then converting the decimal to a percent. Since $125 divided by $225 is 0.5555..., the percent budgeted towards college savings is approximately 56%. Therefore, choice C is correct.

How to Overcome Test Anxiety

Just the thought of taking a test is enough to make most people a little nervous. A test is an important event that can have a long-term impact on your future, so it's important to take it seriously and it's natural to feel anxious about performing well. But just because anxiety is normal, that doesn't mean that it's helpful in test taking, or that you should simply accept it as part of your life. Anxiety can have a variety of effects. These effects can be mild, like making you feel slightly nervous, or severe, like blocking your ability to focus or remember even a simple detail.

If you experience test anxiety—whether severe or mild—it's important to know how to beat it. To discover this, first you need to understand what causes test anxiety.

Causes of Test Anxiety

While we often think of anxiety as an uncontrollable emotional state, it can actually be caused by simple, practical things. One of the most common causes of test anxiety is that a person does not feel adequately prepared for their test. This feeling can be the result of many different issues such as poor study habits or lack of organization, but the most common culprit is time management. Starting to study too late, failing to organize your study time to cover all of the material, or being distracted while you study will mean that you're not well prepared for the test. This may lead to cramming the night before, which will cause you to be physically and mentally exhausted for the test. Poor time management also contributes to feelings of stress, fear, and hopelessness as you realize you are not well prepared but don't know what to do about it.

Other times, test anxiety is not related to your preparation for the test but comes from unresolved fear. This may be a past failure on a test, or poor performance on tests in general. It may come from comparing yourself to others who seem to be performing better or from the stress of living up to expectations. Anxiety may be driven by fears of the future—how failure on this test would affect your educational and career goals. These fears are often completely irrational, but they can still negatively impact your test performance.

> **Review Video: 3 Reasons You Have Test Anxiety**
> Visit mometrix.com/academy and enter code: 428468

Elements of Test Anxiety

As mentioned earlier, test anxiety is considered to be an emotional state, but it has physical and mental components as well. Sometimes you may not even realize that you are suffering from test anxiety until you notice the physical symptoms. These can include trembling hands, rapid heartbeat, sweating, nausea, and tense muscles. Extreme anxiety may lead to fainting or vomiting. Obviously, any of these symptoms can have a negative impact on testing. It is important to recognize them as soon as they begin to occur so that you can address the problem before it damages your performance.

> **Review Video:** <u>3 Ways to Tell You Have Test Anxiety</u>
> Visit mometrix.com/academy and enter code: 927847

The mental components of test anxiety include trouble focusing and inability to remember learned information. During a test, your mind is on high alert, which can help you recall information and stay focused for an extended period of time. However, anxiety interferes with your mind's natural processes, causing you to blank out, even on the questions you know well. The strain of testing during anxiety makes it difficult to stay focused, especially on a test that may take several hours. Extreme anxiety can take a huge mental toll, making it difficult not only to recall test information but even to understand the test questions or pull your thoughts together.

> **Review Video:** <u>How Test Anxiety Affects Memory</u>
> Visit mometrix.com/academy and enter code: 609003

Effects of Test Anxiety

Test anxiety is like a disease—if left untreated, it will get progressively worse. Anxiety leads to poor performance, and this reinforces the feelings of fear and failure, which in turn lead to poor performances on subsequent tests. It can grow from a mild nervousness to a crippling condition. If allowed to progress, test anxiety can have a big impact on your schooling, and consequently on your future.

Test anxiety can spread to other parts of your life. Anxiety on tests can become anxiety in any stressful situation, and blanking on a test can turn into panicking in a job situation. But fortunately, you don't have to let anxiety rule your testing and determine your grades. There are a number of relatively simple steps you can take to move past anxiety and function normally on a test and in the rest of life.

> **Review Video:** <u>How Test Anxiety Impacts Your Grades</u>
> Visit mometrix.com/academy and enter code: 939819

Physical Steps for Beating Test Anxiety

While test anxiety is a serious problem, the good news is that it can be overcome. It doesn't have to control your ability to think and remember information. While it may take time, you can begin taking steps today to beat anxiety.

Just as your first hint that you may be struggling with anxiety comes from the physical symptoms, the first step to treating it is also physical. Rest is crucial for having a clear, strong mind. If you are tired, it is much easier to give in to anxiety. But if you establish good sleep habits, your body and mind will be ready to perform optimally, without the strain of exhaustion. Additionally, sleeping well helps you to retain information better, so you're more likely to recall the answers when you see the test questions.

Getting good sleep means more than going to bed on time. It's important to allow your brain time to relax. Take study breaks from time to time so it doesn't get overworked, and don't study right before bed. Take time to rest your mind before trying to rest your body, or you may find it difficult to fall asleep.

> **Review Video: The Importance of Sleep for Your Brain**
> Visit mometrix.com/academy and enter code: 319338

Along with sleep, other aspects of physical health are important in preparing for a test. Good nutrition is vital for good brain function. Sugary foods and drinks may give a burst of energy but this burst is followed by a crash, both physically and emotionally. Instead, fuel your body with protein and vitamin-rich foods.

Also, drink plenty of water. Dehydration can lead to headaches and exhaustion, especially if your brain is already under stress from the rigors of the test. Particularly if your test is a long one, drink water during the breaks. And if possible, take an energy-boosting snack to eat between sections.

> **Review Video: How Diet Can Affect your Mood**
> Visit mometrix.com/academy and enter code: 624317

Along with sleep and diet, a third important part of physical health is exercise. Maintaining a steady workout schedule is helpful, but even taking 5-minute study breaks to walk can help get your blood pumping faster and clear your head. Exercise also releases endorphins, which contribute to a positive feeling and can help combat test anxiety.

When you nurture your physical health, you are also contributing to your mental health. If your body is healthy, your mind is much more likely to be healthy as well. So take time to rest, nourish your body with healthy food and water, and get moving as much as possible. Taking these physical steps will make you stronger and more able to take the mental steps necessary to overcome test anxiety.

> **Review Video: How to Stay Healthy and Prevent Test Anxiety**
> Visit mometrix.com/academy and enter code: 877894

Mental Steps for Beating Test Anxiety

Working on the mental side of test anxiety can be more challenging, but as with the physical side, there are clear steps you can take to overcome it. As mentioned earlier, test anxiety often stems from lack of preparation, so the obvious solution is to prepare for the test. Effective studying may be the most important weapon you have for beating test anxiety, but you can and should employ several other mental tools to combat fear.

First, boost your confidence by reminding yourself of past success—tests or projects that you aced. If you're putting as much effort into preparing for this test as you did for those, there's no reason you should expect to fail here. Work hard to prepare; then trust your preparation.

Second, surround yourself with encouraging people. It can be helpful to find a study group, but be sure that the people you're around will encourage a positive attitude. If you spend time with others who are anxious or cynical, this will only contribute to your own anxiety. Look for others who are motivated to study hard from a desire to succeed, not from a fear of failure.

Third, reward yourself. A test is physically and mentally tiring, even without anxiety, and it can be helpful to have something to look forward to. Plan an activity following the test, regardless of the outcome, such as going to a movie or getting ice cream.

When you are taking the test, if you find yourself beginning to feel anxious, remind yourself that you know the material. Visualize successfully completing the test. Then take a few deep, relaxing breaths and return to it. Work through the questions carefully but with confidence, knowing that you are capable of succeeding.

Developing a healthy mental approach to test taking will also aid in other areas of life. Test anxiety affects more than just the actual test—it can be damaging to your mental health and even contribute to depression. It's important to beat test anxiety before it becomes a problem for more than testing.

> **Review Video: Test Anxiety and Depression**
> Visit mometrix.com/academy and enter code: 904704

Study Strategy

Being prepared for the test is necessary to combat anxiety, but what does being prepared look like? You may study for hours on end and still not feel prepared. What you need is a strategy for test prep. The next few pages outline our recommended steps to help you plan out and conquer the challenge of preparation.

Step 1: Scope Out the Test

Learn everything you can about the format (multiple choice, essay, etc.) and what will be on the test. Gather any study materials, course outlines, or sample exams that may be available. Not only will this help you to prepare, but knowing what to expect can help to alleviate test anxiety.

Step 2: Map Out the Material

Look through the textbook or study guide and make note of how many chapters or sections it has. Then divide these over the time you have. For example, if a book has 15 chapters and you have five days to study, you need to cover three chapters each day. Even better, if you have the time, leave an extra day at the end for overall review after you have gone through the material in depth.

If time is limited, you may need to prioritize the material. Look through it and make note of which sections you think you already have a good grasp on, and which need review. While you are studying, skim quickly through the familiar sections and take more time on the challenging parts. Write out your plan so you don't get lost as you go. Having a written plan also helps you feel more in control of the study, so anxiety is less likely to arise from feeling overwhelmed at the amount to cover. A sample plan may look like this:

- Day 1: Skim chapters 1–4, study chapter 5 (especially pages 31–33)
- Day 2: Study chapters 6–7, skim chapters 8–9
- Day 3: Skim chapter 10, study chapters 11–12 (especially pages 87–90)
- Day 4: Study chapters 13–15
- Day 5: Overall review (focus most on chapters 5, 6, and 12), take practice test

Step 3: Gather Your Tools

Decide what study method works best for you. Do you prefer to highlight in the book as you study and then go back over the highlighted portions? Or do you type out notes of the important information? Or is it helpful to make flashcards that you can carry with you? Assemble the pens, index cards, highlighters, post-it notes, and any other materials you may need so you won't be distracted by getting up to find things while you study.

If you're having a hard time retaining the information or organizing your notes, experiment with different methods. For example, try color-coding by subject with colored pens, highlighters, or post-it notes. If you learn better by hearing, try recording yourself reading your notes so you can listen while in the car, working out, or simply sitting at your desk. Ask a friend to quiz you from your flashcards, or try teaching someone the material to solidify it in your mind.

Step 4: Create Your Environment

It's important to avoid distractions while you study. This includes both the obvious distractions like visitors and the subtle distractions like an uncomfortable chair (or a too-comfortable couch that makes you want to fall asleep). Set up the best study environment possible: good lighting and a comfortable work area. If background music helps you focus, you may want to turn it on, but otherwise keep the room quiet. If you are using a computer to take notes, be sure you don't have any other windows open, especially applications like social media, games, or anything else that could distract you. Silence your phone and turn off notifications. Be sure to keep water close by so you stay hydrated while you study (but avoid unhealthy drinks and snacks).

Also, take into account the best time of day to study. Are you freshest first thing in the morning? Try to set aside some time then to work through the material. Is your mind clearer in the afternoon or evening? Schedule your study session then. Another method is to study at the same time of day that you will take the test, so that your brain gets used to working on the material at that time and will be ready to focus at test time.

Step 5: Study!

Once you have done all the study preparation, it's time to settle into the actual studying. Sit down, take a few moments to settle your mind so you can focus, and begin to follow your study plan. Don't give in to distractions or let yourself procrastinate. This is your time to prepare so you'll be ready to fearlessly approach the test. Make the most of the time and stay focused.

Of course, you don't want to burn out. If you study too long you may find that you're not retaining the information very well. Take regular study breaks. For example, taking five minutes out of every hour to walk briskly, breathing deeply and swinging your arms, can help your mind stay fresh.

As you get to the end of each chapter or section, it's a good idea to do a quick review. Remind yourself of what you learned and work on any difficult parts. When you feel that you've mastered the material, move on to the next part. At the end of your study session, briefly skim through your notes again.

But while review is helpful, cramming last minute is NOT. If at all possible, work ahead so that you won't need to fit all your study into the last day. Cramming overloads your brain with more information than it can process and retain, and your tired mind may struggle to recall even previously learned information when it is overwhelmed with last-minute study. Also, the urgent nature of cramming and the stress placed on your brain contribute to anxiety. You'll be more likely to go to the test feeling unprepared and having trouble thinking clearly.

So don't cram, and don't stay up late before the test, even just to review your notes at a leisurely pace. Your brain needs rest more than it needs to go over the information again. In fact, plan to finish your studies by noon or early afternoon the day before the test. Give your brain the rest of the day to relax or focus on other things, and get a good night's sleep. Then you will be fresh for the test and better able to recall what you've studied.

Step 6: Take a practice test

Many courses offer sample tests, either online or in the study materials. This is an excellent resource to check whether you have mastered the material, as well as to prepare for the test format and environment.

Check the test format ahead of time: the number of questions, the type (multiple choice, free response, etc.), and the time limit. Then create a plan for working through them. For example, if you have 30 minutes to take a 60-question test, your limit is 30 seconds per question. Spend less time on the questions you know well so that you can take more time on the difficult ones.

If you have time to take several practice tests, take the first one open book, with no time limit. Work through the questions at your own pace and make sure you fully understand them. Gradually work up to taking a test under test conditions: sit at a desk with all study materials put away and set a timer. Pace yourself to make sure you finish the test with time to spare and go back to check your answers if you have time.

After each test, check your answers. On the questions you missed, be sure you understand why you missed them. Did you misread the question (tests can use tricky wording)? Did you forget the information? Or was it something you hadn't learned? Go back and study any shaky areas that the practice tests reveal.

Taking these tests not only helps with your grade, but also aids in combating test anxiety. If you're already used to the test conditions, you're less likely to worry about it, and working through tests until you're scoring well gives you a confidence boost. Go through the practice tests until you feel comfortable, and then you can go into the test knowing that you're ready for it.

Test Tips

On test day, you should be confident, knowing that you've prepared well and are ready to answer the questions. But aside from preparation, there are several test day strategies you can employ to maximize your performance.

First, as stated before, get a good night's sleep the night before the test (and for several nights before that, if possible). Go into the test with a fresh, alert mind rather than staying up late to study.

Try not to change too much about your normal routine on the day of the test. It's important to eat a nutritious breakfast, but if you normally don't eat breakfast at all, consider eating just a protein bar. If you're a coffee drinker, go ahead and have your normal coffee. Just make sure you time it so that the caffeine doesn't wear off right in the middle of your test. Avoid sugary beverages, and drink enough water to stay hydrated but not so much that you need a restroom break 10 minutes into the test. If your test isn't first thing in the morning, consider going for a walk or doing a light workout before the test to get your blood flowing.

Allow yourself enough time to get ready, and leave for the test with plenty of time to spare so you won't have the anxiety of scrambling to arrive in time. Another reason to be early is to select a good seat. It's helpful to sit away from doors and windows, which can be distracting. Find a good seat, get out your supplies, and settle your mind before the test begins.

When the test begins, start by going over the instructions carefully, even if you already know what to expect. Make sure you avoid any careless mistakes by following the directions.

Then begin working through the questions, pacing yourself as you've practiced. If you're not sure on an answer, don't spend too much time on it, and don't let it shake your confidence. Either skip it and come back later, or eliminate as many wrong answers as possible and guess among the remaining ones. Don't dwell on these questions as you continue—put them out of your mind and focus on what lies ahead.

Be sure to read all of the answer choices, even if you're sure the first one is the right answer. Sometimes you'll find a better one if you keep reading. But don't second-guess yourself if you do immediately know the answer. Your gut instinct is usually right. Don't let test anxiety rob you of the information you know.

If you have time at the end of the test (and if the test format allows), go back and review your answers. Be cautious about changing any, since your first instinct tends to be correct, but make sure you didn't misread any of the questions or accidentally mark the wrong answer choice. Look over any you skipped and make an educated guess.

At the end, leave the test feeling confident. You've done your best, so don't waste time worrying about your performance or wishing you could change anything. Instead, celebrate the successful completion of this test. And finally, use this test to learn how to deal with anxiety even better next time.

> **Review Video:** <u>5 Tips to Beat Test Anxiety</u>
> Visit mometrix.com/academy and enter code: 570656

Important Qualification

Not all anxiety is created equal. If your test anxiety is causing major issues in your life beyond the classroom or testing center, or if you are experiencing troubling physical symptoms related to your anxiety, it may be a sign of a serious physiological or psychological condition. If this sounds like your situation, we strongly encourage you to seek professional help.

How to Overcome Your Fear of Math

The word *math* is enough to strike fear into most hearts. How many of us have memories of sitting through confusing lectures, wrestling over mind-numbing homework, or taking tests that still seem incomprehensible even after hours of study? Years after graduation, many still shudder at these memories.

The fact is, math is not just a classroom subject. It has real-world implications that you face every day, whether you realize it or not. This may be balancing your monthly budget, deciding how many supplies to buy for a project, or simply splitting a meal check with friends. The idea of daily confrontations with math can be so paralyzing that some develop a condition known as *math anxiety*.

But you do NOT need to be paralyzed by this anxiety! In fact, while you may have thought all your life that you're not good at math, or that your brain isn't wired to understand it, the truth is that you may have been conditioned to think this way. From your earliest school days, the way you were taught affected the way you viewed different subjects. And the way math has been taught has changed.

Several decades ago, there was a shift in American math classrooms. The focus changed from traditional problem-solving to a conceptual view of topics, de-emphasizing the importance of learning the basics and building on them. The solid foundation necessary for math progression and confidence was undermined. Math became more of a vague concept than a concrete idea. Today, it is common to think of math, not as a straightforward system, but as a mysterious, complicated method that can't be fully understood unless you're a genius.

This is why you may still have nightmares about being called on to answer a difficult problem in front of the class. Math anxiety is a very real, though unnecessary, fear.

Math anxiety may begin with a single class period. Let's say you missed a day in 6th grade math and never quite understood the concept that was taught while you were gone. Since math is cumulative, with each new concept building on past ones, this could very well affect the rest of your math career. Without that one day's knowledge, it will be difficult to understand any other concepts that link to it. Rather than realizing that you're just missing one key piece, you may begin to believe that you're simply not capable of understanding math.

This belief can change the way you approach other classes, career options, and everyday life experiences, if you become anxious at the thought that math might be required. A student who loves science may choose a different path of study upon realizing that multiple math classes will be required for a degree. An aspiring medical student may hesitate at the thought of going through the necessary math classes. For some this anxiety escalates into a more extreme state known as *math phobia*.

Math anxiety is challenging to address because it is rooted deeply and may come from a variety of causes: an embarrassing moment in class, a teacher who did not explain concepts well and contributed to a shaky foundation, or a failed test that contributed to the belief of math failure.

These causes add up over time, encouraged by society's popular view that math is hard and unpleasant. Eventually a person comes to firmly believe that he or she is simply bad at math. This belief makes it difficult to grasp new concepts or even remember old ones. Homework and test grades begin to slip, which only confirms the belief. The poor performance is not due to lack of ability but is caused by math anxiety.

Math anxiety is an emotional issue, not a lack of intelligence. But when it becomes deeply rooted, it can become more than just an emotional problem. Physical symptoms appear. Blood pressure may rise and heartbeat may quicken at the sight of a math problem – or even the thought of math! This fear leads to a mental block. When someone with math anxiety is asked to perform a calculation, even a basic problem can seem overwhelming and impossible. The emotional and physical response to the thought of math prevents the brain from working through it logically.

The more this happens, the more a person's confidence drops, and the more math anxiety is generated. This vicious cycle must be broken!

The first step in breaking the cycle is to go back to very beginning and make sure you really understand the basics of how math works and why it works. It is not enough to memorize rules for multiplication and division. If you don't know WHY these rules work, your foundation will be shaky and you will be at risk of developing a phobia. Understanding mathematical concepts not only promotes confidence and security, but allows you to build on this understanding for new concepts. Additionally, you can solve unfamiliar problems using familiar concepts and processes.

Why is it that students in other countries regularly outperform American students in math? The answer likely boils down to a couple of things: the foundation of mathematical conceptual understanding and societal perception. While students in the US are not expected to *like* or *get* math, in many other nations, students are expected not only to understand math but also to excel at it.

Changing the American view of math that leads to math anxiety is a monumental task. It requires changing the training of teachers nationwide, from kindergarten through high school, so that they learn to teach the *why* behind math and to combat the wrong math views that students may develop. It also involves changing the stigma associated with math, so that it is no longer viewed as unpleasant and incomprehensible. While these are necessary changes, they are challenging and will take time. But in the meantime, math anxiety is not irreversible—it can be faced and defeated, one person at a time.

False Beliefs

One reason math anxiety has taken such hold is that several false beliefs have been created and shared until they became widely accepted. Some of these unhelpful beliefs include the following:

There is only one way to solve a math problem. In the same way that you can choose from different driving routes and still arrive at the same house, you can solve a math problem using different methods and still find the correct answer. A person who understands the reasoning behind math calculations may be able to look at an unfamiliar concept and find the right answer, just by applying logic to the knowledge they already have. This approach may be different than what is taught in the classroom, but it is still valid. Unfortunately, even many teachers view math as a subject where the best course of action is to memorize the rule or process for each problem rather than as a place for students to exercise logic and creativity in finding a solution.

Many people don't have a mind for math. A person who has struggled due to poor teaching or math anxiety may falsely believe that he or she doesn't have the mental capacity to grasp mathematical concepts. Most of the time, this is false. Many people find that when they are relieved of their math anxiety, they have more than enough brainpower to understand math.

Men are naturally better at math than women. Even though research has shown this to be false, many young women still avoid math careers and classes because of their belief that their math abilities are inferior. Many girls have come to believe that math is a male skill and have given up trying to understand or enjoy it.

Counting aids are bad. Something like counting on your fingers or drawing out a problem to visualize it may be frowned on as childish or a crutch, but these devices can help you get a tangible understanding of a problem or a concept.

Sadly, many students buy into these ideologies at an early age. A young girl who enjoys math class may be conditioned to think that she doesn't actually have the brain for it because math is for boys, and may turn her energies to other pursuits, permanently closing the door on a wide range of opportunities. A child who finds the right answer but doesn't follow the teacher's method may believe that he is doing it wrong and isn't good at math. A student who never had a problem with math before may have a poor teacher and become confused, yet believe that the problem is because she doesn't have a mathematical mind.

Students who have bought into these erroneous beliefs quickly begin to add their own anxieties, adapting them to their own personal situations:

I'll never use this in real life. A huge number of people wrongly believe that math is irrelevant outside the classroom. By adopting this mindset, they are handicapping themselves for a life in a mathematical world, as well as limiting their career choices. When they are inevitably faced with real-world math, they are conditioning themselves to respond with anxiety.

I'm not quick enough. While timed tests and quizzes, or even simply comparing yourself with other students in the class, can lead to this belief, speed is not an indicator of skill level. A person can work very slowly yet understand at a deep level.

If I can understand it, it's too easy. People with a low view of their own abilities tend to think that if they are able to grasp a concept, it must be simple. They cannot accept the idea that they are capable of understanding math. This belief will make it harder to learn, no matter how intelligent they are.

I just can't learn this. An overwhelming number of people think this, from young children to adults, and much of the time it is simply not true. But this mindset can turn into a self-fulfilling prophecy that keeps you from exercising and growing your math ability.

The good news is, each of these myths can be debunked. For most people, they are based on emotion and psychology, NOT on actual ability! It will take time, effort, and the desire to change, but change is possible. Even if you have spent years thinking that you don't have the capability to understand math, it is not too late to uncover your true ability and find relief from the anxiety that surrounds math.

Math Strategies

It is important to have a plan of attack to combat math anxiety. There are many useful strategies for pinpointing the fears or myths and eradicating them:

Go back to the basics. For most people, math anxiety stems from a poor foundation. You may think that you have a complete understanding of addition and subtraction, or even decimals and percentages, but make absolutely sure. Learning math is different from learning other subjects. For example, when you learn history, you study various time periods and places and events. It may be important to memorize dates or find out about the lives of famous people. When you move from US history to world history, there will be some overlap, but a large amount of the information will be new. Mathematical concepts, on the other hand, are very closely linked and highly dependent on each other. It's like climbing a ladder – if a rung is missing from your understanding, it may be difficult or impossible for you to climb any higher, no matter how hard you try. So go back and make sure your math foundation is strong. This may mean taking a remedial math course, going to a tutor to work through the shaky concepts, or just going through your old homework to make sure you really understand it.

Speak the language. Math has a large vocabulary of terms and phrases unique to working problems. Sometimes these are completely new terms, and sometimes they are common words, but are used differently in a math setting. If you can't speak the language, it will be very difficult to get a thorough understanding of the concepts. It's common for students to think that they don't understand math when they simply don't understand the vocabulary. The good news is that this is fairly easy to fix. Brushing up on any terms you aren't quite sure of can help bring the rest of the concepts into focus.

Check your anxiety level. When you think about math, do you feel nervous or uncomfortable? Do you struggle with feelings of inadequacy, even on concepts that you know you've already learned? It's important to understand your specific math anxieties, and what triggers them. When you catch yourself falling back on a false belief, mentally replace it with the truth. Don't let yourself believe that you can't learn, or that struggling with a concept means you'll never understand it. Instead, remind yourself of how much you've already learned and dwell on that past success. Visualize grasping the new concept, linking it to your old knowledge, and moving on to the next challenge. Also, learn how to manage anxiety when it arises. There are many techniques for coping with the irrational fears that rise to the surface when you enter the math classroom. This may include controlled breathing, replacing negative thoughts with positive ones, or visualizing success. Anxiety interferes with your ability to concentrate and absorb information, which in turn contributes to greater anxiety. If you can learn how to regain control of your thinking, you will be better able to pay attention, make progress, and succeed!

Don't go it alone. Like any deeply ingrained belief, math anxiety is not easy to eradicate. And there is no need for you to wrestle through it on your own. It will take time, and many people find that speaking with a counselor or psychiatrist helps. They can help you develop strategies for responding to anxiety and overcoming old ideas. Additionally, it can be very helpful to take a short course or seek out a math tutor to help you find and fix the missing rungs on your ladder and make sure that you're ready to progress to the next level. You can also find a number of math aids online: courses that will teach you mental devices for figuring out problems, how to get the most out of your math classes, etc.

Check your math attitude. No matter how much you want to learn and overcome your anxiety, you'll have trouble if you still have a negative attitude toward math. If you think it's too hard, or just have general feelings of dread about math, it will be hard to learn and to break through the anxiety. Work on cultivating a positive math attitude. Remind yourself that math is not just a hurdle to be cleared, but a valuable asset. When you view math with a positive attitude, you'll be much more likely to understand and even enjoy it. This is something you must do for yourself. You may find it helpful to visit with a counselor. Your tutor, friends, and family may cheer you on in your endeavors. But your greatest asset is yourself. You are inside your own mind – tell yourself what you need to hear. Relive past victories. Remind yourself that you are capable of understanding math. Root out any false beliefs that linger and replace them with positive truths. Even if it doesn't feel true at first, it will begin to affect your thinking and pave the way for a positive, anxiety-free mindset.

Aside from these general strategies, there are a number of specific practical things you can do to begin your journey toward overcoming math anxiety. Something as simple as learning a new note-taking strategy can change the way you approach math and give you more confidence and understanding. New study techniques can also make a huge difference.

Math anxiety leads to bad habits. If it causes you to be afraid of answering a question in class, you may gravitate toward the back row. You may be embarrassed to ask for help. And you may procrastinate on assignments, which leads to rushing through them at the last moment when it's too late to get a better understanding. It's important to identify your negative behaviors and replace them with positive ones:

Prepare ahead of time. Read the lesson before you go to class. Being exposed to the topics that will be covered in class ahead of time, even if you don't understand them perfectly, is extremely helpful in increasing what you retain from the lecture. Do your homework and, if you're still shaky, go over some extra problems. The key to a solid understanding of math is practice.

Sit front and center. When you can easily see and hear, you'll understand more, and you'll avoid the distractions of other students if no one is in front of you. Plus, you're more likely to be sitting with students who are positive and engaged, rather than others with math anxiety. Let their positive math attitude rub off on you.

Ask questions in class and out. If you don't understand something, just ask. If you need a more in-depth explanation, the teacher may need to work with you outside of class, but often it's a simple concept you don't quite understand, and a single question may clear it up. If you wait, you may not be able to follow the rest of the day's lesson. For extra help, most professors have office hours outside of class when you can go over concepts one-on-one to clear up any uncertainties. Additionally, there may be a *math lab* or study session you can attend for homework help. Take advantage of this.

Review. Even if you feel that you've fully mastered a concept, review it periodically to reinforce it. Going over an old lesson has several benefits: solidifying your understanding, giving you a confidence boost, and even giving some new insights into material that you're currently learning! Don't let yourself get rusty. That can lead to problems with learning later concepts.

Teaching Tips

While the math student's mindset is the most crucial to overcoming math anxiety, it is also important for others to adjust their math attitudes. Teachers and parents have an enormous influence on how students relate to math. They can either contribute to math confidence or math anxiety.

As a parent or teacher, it is very important to convey a positive math attitude. Retelling horror stories of your own bad experience with math will contribute to a new generation of math anxiety. Even if you don't share your experiences, others will be able to sense your fears and may begin to believe them.

Even a careless comment can have a big impact, so watch for phrases like *He's not good at math* or *I never liked math*. You are a crucial role model, and your children or students will unconsciously adopt your mindset. Give them a positive example to follow. Rather than teaching them to fear the math world before they even know it, teach them about all its potential and excitement.

Work to present math as an integral, beautiful, and understandable part of life. Encourage creativity in solving problems. Watch for false beliefs and dispel them. Cross the lines between subjects: integrate history, English, and music with math. Show students how math is used every day, and how the entire world is based on mathematical principles, from the pull of gravity to the shape of seashells. Instead of letting students see math as a necessary evil, direct them to view it as an imaginative, beautiful art form – an art form that they are capable of mastering and using.

Don't give too narrow a view of math. It is more than just numbers. Yes, working problems and learning formulas is a large part of classroom math. But don't let the teaching stop there. Teach students about the everyday implications of math. Show them how nature works according to the laws of mathematics, and take them outside to make discoveries of their own. Expose them to math-related careers by inviting visiting speakers, asking students to do research and presentations, and learning students' interests and aptitudes on a personal level.

Demonstrate the importance of math. Many people see math as nothing more than a required stepping stone to their degree, a nuisance with no real usefulness. Teach students that algebra is used every day in managing their bank accounts, in following recipes, and in scheduling the day's events. Show them how learning to do geometric proofs helps them to develop logical thinking, an invaluable life skill. Let them see that math surrounds them and is integrally linked to their daily lives: that weather predictions are based on math, that math was used to design cars and other machines, etc. Most of all, give them the tools to use math to enrich their lives.

Make math as tangible as possible. Use visual aids and objects that can be touched. It is much easier to grasp a concept when you can hold it in your hands and manipulate it, rather than just listening to the lecture. Encourage math outside of the classroom. The real world is full of measuring, counting, and calculating, so let students participate in this. Keep your eyes open for numbers and patterns to discuss. Talk about how scores are calculated in sports games and how far apart plants are placed in a garden row for maximum growth. Build the mindset that math is a normal and interesting part of daily life.

Finally, find math resources that help to build a positive math attitude. There are a number of books that show math as fascinating and exciting while teaching important concepts, for example: *The Math Curse; A Wrinkle in Time; The Phantom Tollbooth;* and *Fractals, Googols and Other Mathematical Tales*. You can also find a number of online resources: math puzzles and games, videos that show math in nature, and communities of math enthusiasts. On a local level, students can compete in a variety of math competitions with other schools or join a math club.

The student who experiences math as exciting and interesting is unlikely to suffer from math anxiety. Going through life without this handicap is an immense advantage and opens many doors that others have closed through their fear.

Self-Check

Whether you suffer from math anxiety or not, chances are that you have been exposed to some of the false beliefs mentioned above. Now is the time to check yourself for any errors you may have accepted. Do you think you're not wired for math? Or that you don't need to understand it since you're not planning on a math career? Do you think math is just too difficult for the average person?

Find the errors you've taken to heart and replace them with positive thinking. Are you capable of learning math? Yes! Can you control your anxiety? Yes! These errors will resurface from time to time, so be watchful. Don't let others with math anxiety influence you or sway your confidence. If you're having trouble with a concept, find help. Don't let it discourage you!

Create a plan of attack for defeating math anxiety and sharpening your skills. Do some research and decide if it would help you to take a class, get a tutor, or find some online resources to fine-tune your knowledge. Make the effort to get good nutrition, hydration, and sleep so that you are operating at full capacity. Remind yourself daily that you are skilled and that anxiety does not control you. Your mind is capable of so much more than you know. Give it the tools it needs to grow and thrive.

Thank You

We at Mometrix would like to extend our heartfelt thanks to you, our friend and patron, for allowing us to play a part in your journey. It is a privilege to serve people from all walks of life who are unified in their commitment to building the best future they can for themselves.

The preparation you devote to these important testing milestones may be the most valuable educational opportunity you have for making a real difference in your life. We encourage you to put your heart into it—that feeling of succeeding, overcoming, and yes, conquering will be well worth the hours you've invested.

We want to hear your story, your struggles and your successes, and if you see any opportunities for us to improve our materials so we can help others even more effectively in the future, please share that with us as well. **The team at Mometrix would be absolutely thrilled to hear from you!** So please, send us an email (support@mometrix.com) and let's stay in touch.

If you'd like some additional help, check out these other resources we offer for your exam:

http://MometrixFlashcards.com/STAAR

Additional Bonus Material

Due to our efforts to try to keep this book to a manageable length, we've created a link that will give you access to all of your additional bonus material.

Please visit https://www.mometrix.com/bonus948/staarg7math to access the information.